To Walk a Country Mile

To Walk a Country Mile

Reflections of a life in rural Canada

BY MARY ELIZABETH MAXWELL

MOULIN

Copyright © 1997 by Moulin Publishing Limited/Mary Elizabeth Maxwell

All rights reserved. No part of this book may be used or reproduced in any manner whatsoever without prior permission of the publisher.

Moulin Publishing Limited
P.O. Box #560
Norval, Ontario
Canada L0P 1K0

Canadian Cataloguing in Publication Data

Maxwell, Mary Elizabeth, 1914-
    To walk a country mile: reflections of a life in rural Canada

ISBN 1-896867-03-0

1. Norval (Ont.) – History – Anecdotes.   I. Title.

FC3099.N693M39 1997   971.3'533   C97-901111-6
F1059.5.N86M39 1997

Printed and bound in Canada

1 2 3 4 5 ML 00 99 98 97

Cover and text design by Andrew Smith Graphics Inc.
Front cover photograph by Mary Elizabeth Maxwell

*For my parents, Charlie and Mame,
who loved their home and their community
and were good neighbours to all.*

Contents

Acknowledgements 9

Introduction 11

CHAPTER ONE
Early Settling History 12

CHAPTER TWO
The Village 28

CHAPTER THREE
Growing Up in Norval 58

CHAPTER FOUR
The Depression Years 76

CHAPTER FIVE
A Life on the Farm 94

CHAPTER SIX
The Community Beyond Norval Village 124

CHAPTER SEVEN
Old Timers Remembered 136

CHAPTER EIGHT
The Fabric of the Community 160

CHAPTER NINE
The Pioneers Live On 172

Acknowledgements

With gratitude and appreciation, we say "Thank you" to the many people who helped us put this outline of history together by sharing memories long past but never forgotten.

To Ed Boyce and his nephew Chris Boyce, who have warmed an aging heart by putting a cover on her book, and to Kelly Crawford who fine-tuned the manuscript with patience and understanding. They have all become our "extended family". Such a nice feeling.

To Norman Holt who foresaw the makings of a book (while some history was still alive and well).

To Ray and Bernice Whaley, Bruce McNab, Ralph Forster, Geoffrey and Donald Noble, Clarence Hunter, Julian Reed, M.P. Lloyd Hustler and Gayle Lyons, for writing up their own families' comings and goings. To Mark Rowe, for the Kingston Norval clippings.

To Ross and Lil Garbutt, Joy Laird, Dorothy (Watson) McLean, Jim Clark, Heather Eccles, Betty (van Vliet) Millenaar, and the late Dr. Ethel (Noble) Dempsey, for pictures.

To Elizabeth Grant for Union Church information and Depression prices.

To Elaine Robinson-Bertrand for the pioneer road map.

To Joan (Browne) Carter for her extensive research on the lists of Veterans in the two World Wars.

To Barbara Coupland, Kate McColman, Joe Harris and Maureen Newns for school memories.

To my husband, Jimmie Maxwell, for his unfailing support and to my daughters, Laurie and Mary Honey who said, "Write it down Mother, you always wanted to do it!"

Thank you everyone!

Introduction

Driving in the Caledon Hills some years ago, my husband and I were confused by several detours and a washed-out culvert and were losing our bearings when we spied a lone man standing on the side of the road. I rolled the window down and asked him "Where does this road take you?" He smiled, looked up the road, down the road, then turned to us and said "It takes you lots of places, and if yer goin' to Erin kin I go with you?" So he climbed in the back seat and we started off, no wiser than before. Eventually we stumbled on Erin, where our travelling companion thanked us kindly for the ride. We left him standing on the sidewalk, still smiling.

This "country mile" ahead of you will take you lots of places too, never very far from home; the direction, like the mileage, is uncertain, time is of no consequence, visits here and there are taken for granted, and detours often occur. When I undertook to walk that mile with my pen, it started out to be a once-over-lightly account of life on the home farm and the village and community of Norval as it was when I was growing up. However, I soon realized that this area is so rich in historical significance that I could only skim the surface. A hundred years ago this community with the village as its center was fairly typical of rural, small-town Ontario, but the settlement has always had a particularly unique character. Now, a hundred years later, the identity of the community and village of Norval is threatened on every side, and only by keeping some of the past alive can we hope to retain any part of that unique quality for the next generation.

CHAPTER ONE
Early Settling History

*Norval circa 1870.
Robert Noble's house is in the background. My grandmother, Mary Noble is one of the figures in the meadow, the small boy is Alex Noble. The poles on the horizon are the trunks of pine trees, killed in order to clear the land for farming.*

Early Settling History

THE MCNABS OF NORVAL

The McNab family history as it relates to the Norval area could have been written time and time again throughout Southern Ontario. So many of the early settlers came up from New England into unknown territory covered with bush, and at great personal cost carved out a new life for their families in the Canadian Wilderness.

James McNab, (born 1787 – died 1866) the second son of John (1758–1846) and Janet Fletcher, (1763–1811) left Barnet, Vermont, for Upper Canada. James enlisted with the York Volunteers and fought in the War of 1812 in defence of Fort George and Queenston Heights under General Brock. He attained the rank of Lieutenant.

After the war he stayed in Upper Canada and married Sarah Marsh, (1790–1866). A son, James was born in 1817 in Toronto Township which at that time was part of the Home District but in 1852 became part of Peel County. James was joined by his brother Alexander and his wife Jean Shaw, his sister Janet and her husband James McLeran, and another brother, Archibald. All arrived before 1823.

The second purchase of Mississauga land from the native Indians in 1818 had reserved a two-mile strip along the Credit River for the exclusive use of the Indians, but in 1820 that reservation was lifted and the McNabs acquired land on the Credit in the east portion of Esquesing Township. Esquesing at that time was part of the Gore District, but in 1853 became one of the Townships in the new Halton County where settlement had started in 1783. By 1817 there were 6,684 residents, mostly United Empire Loyalists, settled along the shore of Lake Ontario, the Southern boundary of Halton County.

Archibald McNab,
1801-1870

Not until 1819 did settlement begin in Esquesing, which was the northeast township. By 1821, when the first Town meeting was called to choose local officials, the population was 424 souls. A "fish road" along the Credit was the only connection with the settlement in the South.

The McNabs built a dam on the Credit River to provide water power for a sawmill, later adding a grist mill and woollen mill. Remnants of that first dam at Norval were still visible until Hurricane Hazel took the stones out in 1954. In 1832 a road from York reached the Township. The community which grew up around the mills was called McNabsville until 1836, when a post office, the second in the Township, was opened and the name of the village was changed to Norval. The new name was either a contraction of North Vale, New England, or from a Scottish verse "My name is Norval, along the Grampian hills my father feeds his flocks." At this distance no one can settle the argument.

James McNab became the owner of the mill and about 400 acres of land and is credited with developing the early community. In 1827 he advertised in McKenzie's *Colonial Advocate* encouraging craftsmen and tradesmen to come to his Esquesing Mills. James' life was changed when a millstone crushed his leg and it was amputated above the knee; there was no anesthetic in those days, just lots of whisky, and then tar on the wound. On a visit to England later he was fitted with a very functional prosthesis.

In 1830 James leased the mill to John Barnhart, but in 1834 resumed management himself.

During the 1837 Rebellion James raised and equipped a militia unit at his own expense. John Leslie of Glen Williams served under him. When James asked for compensation from the Rebellion Losses Bill he was refused, so in 1838 he sold his mills to General Sir Peter Adamson.

In 1847 James McNab sold his land in and around Norval to his brother Alexander and then moved to Owen Sound.

In 1854 Alexander sold the lands to General Adamson who already had the mills, but Alexander reserved Lots 5 and 11 in the village, a piece of pasture land and the burial ground which James had established on a hill overlooking the village. In the *Historical*

Jane Campbell McNab, wife of Archibald, 1816-1880

Atlas of Halton County of 1877, the plan of Norval shows the burial ground as Lots 354 and 360, between Esquesing and Chinguacousy Townships. Among the many pioneers buried on this site were Alexander's infant son in 1823, and later Alexander, his wife Jean and his father John. At the time of writing it is understood that graves have been removed to the present Norval Hillcrest Cemetery and discussions are under way with regard to the care and upkeep of what remains of the pioneer burying ground.

FISH WALKS AND WAGON TRAILS – ROADS

When the early settlers started coming in to Southern Ontario the surveyors had been there ahead of them, and when those pioneers were given a Crown deed, (a grant of land from the British Government), it stated exactly where they could build a home and start raising crops. There was nothing on that piece of paper to tell them what they could expect: there could be muskeg, moose pasture or marvelous soil, and the settlers would spend years clearing their land.

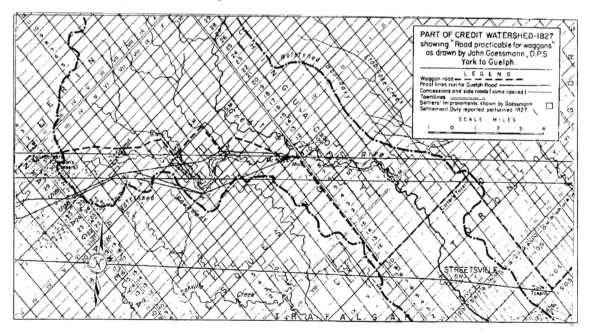

To preserve some law and order in the allocation of settlement, the surveyors laid out a grid with military precision. They marked out counties, each county having four townships. The townships were divided into concessions, the concessions into lots. Lines and sideroads formed connecting links.

Halton County's townships were Esquesing, Trafalgar, Nelson and Nassagaweya.

The townships were separated by township or "Town Lines", and the sideroads were numbered from a "Base" line (again a township border line). Thus Five Sideroad Esquesing was five lots removed from the "Base" and Ten Sideroad was five lots above that and so on. However, in Esquesing and probably in other townships too, the surveyors ran a "check line" of sorts, so we get fifteen sideroad and two lots later, seventeen sideroad and then carry on with twenty-two, twenty-seven, and thirty-two, which finds itself running into Wellington County Base line.

For some reason base lines were always called "line" and ran contrary to the concession lines. In Esquesing the concession lines are measured roughly from west to east, every line 7/8 of a mile apart from the next. In old Trafalgar Township, settled a bit earlier, the concession lines are one mile and 1/8 apart, so when you drive down the ninth Line of Esquesing to the Base Line (now Steeles) you must jog left a quarter of a mile to enter the Ninth line of Trafalgar. The jogs are consistent all across the townships.

A "lot" is usually a square hundred acres but it could also be a "string hundred" with frontages on two lines. String hundreds are a bit awkward to farm, with very long farm lanes and long distances to move the cows between the barn and pasture.

Sometimes you will find a "blind" line which is going nowhere. It started out with good intentions but often ended up as a prelude to a "given road", which seemed to be an easier route to follow, although it did encroach on private property. We have a prime example of that in Norval. The town line between Halton's Esquesing and Peel County's Chinguacousy at one time went directly south across the Credit River and Hunter's flats and came out at Geoff Noble's gate, having skirted Murray Laird's river property. The Credit was shallow on the flats, and teams could ford the river. A bridge was built there but is supposed to have been washed out in the floods. To properly bridge that stretch of flats and allow for the width of the river in flood would have been a huge undertaking, so half a mile above the village the given road curved sideways down the valley hill and the Credit was bridged at a much narrower point.

One of the deepest spots on the river, complete with a whirlpool, was practically under the bridge. As very young children having to cross that bridge to school, we were always warned to walk in the middle of it. "After all," said our Grandfather, "there might be sharks and crocodiles down there."

There is now a sign beside the new bridge of 1991 advising "Dangerous Waters." My mother knew that years ago!

Peel County's Chinguacousy Township was arranged a little differently than Halton's Esquesing Township. Chinguacousy had a Centre Road right down the middle known as Hurontario Street, running from Lake Ontario to Lake Huron and passing through other counties on its way. The concession fanned out from the centre and you will find a First Concession East and West, a Second Concession East and West, and so on, and eventually the Sixth Line West which is also the Eleventh Concession of Esquesing.

Robert Glendinning and his wife Mary (Noble) Glendinning, 1884.

Once you get the hang of it, and providing there are a few road signs here and there to mark the county roads, you can enjoy driving in Ontario and find your way home again. But a complication is creeping in. Chinguacousy is *naming* the lines and sideroads. The Fifth Line West is now Heritage Road, the Fourth Line West is Mississauga Road, Seventeen Sideroad is Mayfield Road, Twentysecond Sideroad is Old School Road and so on.

We'll need updated maps all over Ontario before long! The Town Line at Norval is now officially known as Regional Road Nineteen, Sixth Concession West, Chinguacousy, as Eleventh Concession East, Esquesing (now Halton Hills,) and as Winston Churchill Boulevard. A multiple choice indeed.

Compared to yesteryear's tranquility, the number of new highways streaking across our countryside, sometimes accompanied with battalions of hydro towers, suggests that future generations will have to step smartly to avoid being run over or electrocuted!

That riverside "first walk" the Indians used (see McNab) and the original 'wagon road' (see map) were so much simpler. You just followed footsteps and wheel tracks and didn't worry about the traffic. The early "path masters" with their teams and scrapers laying down plank roads were the men who really opened up the country. The wagon road on the map of 1837 is hard to follow and can only be traced with difficulty.

And just a word to the newcomers in the townships. If your husband comes home from work and says he will "just run around the block before supper", put his supper back in the oven. He is about to run five and three quarter MILES!

Lanterns in the Bush 1895

When my Glenndinning grandparents arrived in Canada in the 1860s, the lighting facilities had already progressed from pine knots in the fireplace to candles to lamps and lanterns, although candle molds were still in use. The tin molds came in groups of four, six or eight; string wicks were held in place and then melted tallow was poured into the mold. When coal oil became available some very elaborate lamps were produced with cranberry shades and china bases. There were bracket lamps to hang on the wall and hanging lamps for the ceiling, which could be raised and lowered on a chain. One such candelabra, now electrified, is hanging in St. Paul's Anglican Church in Norval. In homes the lamps and lanterns were cleaned every day, the wicks were trimmed and the coal oil was topped up. To clean the glass you took it off the lamp, breathed hard into the top so a little moisture would form, and then, holding a crumpled piece of newspaper you carefully put your hand inside from the bottom and polished the glass.

From the mid-1870s to the late 1890s the Glendinnings lived above the village in the Credit Valley. My mother and her sister Sara were involved in many church and community activities and if they were going to be late coming home Grandad would go to meet them with a lantern. That walk along the bush and a stretch of the river was very dark. The McFarlane girls, whose path took them through the West Branch bush, were also met by their Father, and Henry Pettigrew walked down the long hill to meet his daughters. Village life was not necessarily all sweetness and charm and parents were well aware that several young men in the village were not above imposing their company on any of the girls and following them home. One lad bragged about this, and on one occasion he was confronted by my Grandfather carrying a lantern to meet his daughter. As the lad told the story later, perhaps otherwise than truthfully, he said "I kicked the lantern out of Mr. Glendinning's hand and ran away." It was a wise move. My Grandfather was six foot two in his socks and all muscle.

Flashlights appeared around 1885, weighed five pounds and cost $5.00, and were advertised in the papers of the day as "instant light for any room." They heralded the beginning of different means of providing light, although lamps and lanterns continued to be the main source of light for many decades.

> The possibilities of Electricity are apparently boundless, and almost every day brings forth some new invention for its application to useful purposes. One of the latest of these is the Portable Electric Lighter, which is now manufactured in this city, and which is exhibited at No. 22 Water street. This is in effect a small chemical battery, occupying a space of five square inches, and weighing but five pounds, with all its fittings. By pressing upon a knob the current is produced, a strip of platinum is heated to incandescence, and light is instantaneous. This can be carried from room to room and placed upon the desk or the table. At a slight additional expense it can be so arranged as to ring an alarm or signal bell, or to light gas in any part of the house. The contrivance is novel; simple, convenient and cheap.

Robert Noble and the Norval Flour Mill (1868–1919)

Someone asked "Why was a flour mill so important to a settlement in the 1830s?" The answer is simple: the mill put bread on the table, provided a market outlet for the farmers' grain, attracted newcomers to the settlement and gave them employment.

Robert Noble was the youngest son of John and Ann (Warwick) Noble, born in 1835 at Howe Mill in Cumberland, England. The family came to Canada in 1851, landing at Montreal after six weeks at sea, and came on to Dundas by barge. Robert served three years apprenticeship at the Wentworth Mill, then got a chance of one year's schooling in a public school near Carlisle. From there he went on to manage flour mills in Elora and Freelton. Those were the years when the American slaves were making their way north to freedom and on one occasion Robert was startled to find one of them in the mill trying to get warm.

The story is told that one day at Norval, Robert was dressing stones when Colonel Clay, through whom he had bought the property from the Ontario Bank, came along and said "Well, Noble, how do you expect to pay for this property?" The answer was, "By minding my own business."

Robert Noble was a member of the Toronto Board of Trade and the Dominion Millers' Fire Insurance Association, but his primary interests were in his own community at home.

Robert married Marion Laing of Dundas, daughter of a prominent business family there.

In buying the Norval mill, his purchase included a good woollen mill, extensive land holdings and also the mill owner's home, a fine and substantial residence, erected by Sir Peter Adamson. The mill itself, a frame building, needed repairs, and after struggling for eight years with all kinds of difficulties, Mr. Noble shut the mill down and rebuilt it as a four-storey brick structure.

Robert Noble (1835-1910) with his wife Marion (Laing) Noble.

Norval flour mills (circa 1930).

Not only did he end up with a mill that was acknowledged to be one of the finest in the country, but he also restored the integrity of the ownership. Farmers no longer had to leave their loads of grain at the top of the hill and walk down to the office to see if there was enough money in the till to pay them for their grain. A mutual respect developed and under Mr. Noble's guidance the mill prospered. Therefore the village and community prospered too.

The finest grade of flour milled in Norval was "King's Choice" made from western wheat noted for its high gluten content. This Manitoba wheat was shipped to Norval Station by the Grand Trunk Railway and teamed from the station to the mill. Very fine pastry flour, the "National" brand, was milled from Ontario Fall wheat. Both flours were shipped all over Canada and even to the West Indies.

In the early days of milling and up to the 1900s labour-saving devices were few; men were still climbing miles of stairs and lifting tons of flour in barrels. The barrels were made in the cooper shop just behind the mill, and some of the best coopers were the McPherson men. When elevators came on the scene, an endless belt elevator system made of 12-inch, 4-ply rubber belting, confined in a two and a half by six foot shaft, certainly eased the work load.

In 1918 my dad was constructing one of those 40-foot elevator shafts in Acton, and was at the bottom of the shaft when his co-worker, Henry Aurey, yelled in terror from the top. A scantling being lowered had slipped off the rope. Dad looked up and the 4x4 slid down the inside of his face, separating his nose from his cheek. He carried the scars from that injury the rest of his life. Mr. Noble had a second elevator in Acton at that time.

Before the Toronto-Guelph Electric Railway, (the Radial) made its way to Norval and a switchback to the mill was constructed, all the flour was teamed to Norval Station, a mile and a half distant. A full load was 14 barrels, each weighing 200 pounds, but in bad weather when the mud was axle deep the horses could only haul five barrels. The teams were housed in a brick stable which is still there on our home farm. The teamsters were expected to look after the team they drove, have them fed and groomed, harnessed, and ready for the road by 7:00 a.m. The horses certainly earned their oats. In the early years the teams had to use the short, steep, quicksand hill on the old town line which often meant having to keep a standby team to get the load up the hill.

The mill employed twenty-five to thirty men and their hours

The mill in 1917

The mill, mill race and mill sheds, circa 1930.

were regulated by the mill bell. It rang at 7:00 a.m., 12:00 noon, 1:00 p.m. and 6:00 p.m.

Mr. Noble learned the milling trade when runs of stone were used in the grinding of the flour. Later he installed the more progressive roller system which put his mill in the forefront of the flour milling business in Canada at that time.

Robert Noble was highly respected in his home village and in the wider business community, as was his son, Alex, who followed him. Colonel Alexander Noble was in charge of the mill until 1919 when he sold the mill to Mr. W.J. Campbell, who, after trying for over three years to hang on to the mill property and keep up the mortgage payments, finally lost his mill to Mr. W.B. Browne, a grain broker in Toronto.

Flour mills make flour but they also make history, and so often in old Ontario you can trace the footprints of our past by the flour on a miller's feet.

The former mill owner's home, "The Elms" is now occupied

by Robert Noble's great-grandson, Julian Reed, M.P. Every Christmas Julian's sense of tradition leads him to fire up the old brick oven in the wall, and bake a good batch of bread, perhaps twenty loaves or more, which he shares with all who come through the door. My Grandmother, Mary Noble, baked many loaves in that same oven in the late 1860s.

January 29th, 1930

The night we all remember — the night the mill burned down.

The famous Norval Flour Mill, owned for over fifty years by Robert Noble, and for the last seven years by W.G.M. Browne, burned early Tuesday morning, January 29th, 1930. There was a considerable quantity of grain in the mill at the time. The origin of the fire is still unknown. The mill had been temporarily shut down as an ice jam in the Credit River was causing a shortage of water so necessary to the operation of the mill.

The first alarm was sounded by Claudia Greenwood, wife of L.F. Greenwood, manager of the Bank of Nova Scotia, which was just a stone's throw from the mill. Mr. Greenwood alerted Mr. Browne, who ran to the mill in his bare feet and made a desperate attempt to rescue the books in the office. Two people tried to get Mr. Browne out: first, Ray Pomeroy, who was overcome by the smoke and then Norman Brown, who managed to drag the mill owner out to safety. The owner had been badly cut by broken glass when he went through the office window.

The village was saved further losses as the light wind that night was blowing down the river. A dozen families were

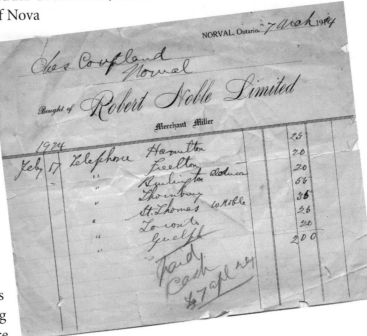

A bill for telephone calls made on the death of Grandmother Glendinning, 1924. Later the same year the family had a phone of their own.

now out of work. The flour mill had provided employment for several generations in some of those families.

My father had worked in the mill as a millwright for several years in Mr. Noble's time and knew the mill well, inside and out. He had always said that when the mill was running, a spark from any source would be disastrous. In Dad's one-line-a-day diary, which he kept most of his working life, the mill fire rated two lines: "sorry to see it go down, fire had to have started on the ground floor to get such a hold." The flames from the mill were so high and so bright that you could see across the country for a mile, and we didn't need the lamp lit in the house. Heroic efforts by the Georgetown and Brampton Fire Brigades saved the grist mill. Before long, Mr. John Slingsby was back on the job grinding chop for farmers.

The pile of scorched grain in the mill burned for weeks. On Easter Sunday morning, 1930, there was still a thin plume of smoke rising from the ashes, and the smell of burnt porridge hung over the valley for months.

The grist mill survived for twenty-four years after the fire destroyed the flour mill, but in 1954 Hurricane Hazel took the end out of it. In the mid 1930s, Gordie Browne, the mill owner's elder son, was able to handle the chopping jobs with help from Mr. Slingsby; when his father died in 1938, Gordie, at about fifteen years of age, took over the gristing work himself and did a good job. The farmers were most appreciative of Gordie's abilities and willingness to help. When Gordie joined the Army in 1942 the grist mill was briefly held by Mr. Tarzwell, followed by a series of renters who used the property for sales and storage. By this time most of the farmers had home grinders and chop for their cattle was not a problem. Various parts of the original mill property changed

Lieutenant-Colonel A. L. Noble, son of Robert, took charge of the mill around 1910 after Robert's death.

hands several times. The flats below the mill but above the tailrace became the site of the Riviera, an entertainment centre.

Since 1920–1921 when # 7 highway was first cut through the village, the highway was moved at least twice, and now runs over the main part of the old mill and also over the mill sheds.

The Norval Flour Mill sat proudly on the Credit River for about one hundred years, but its best days were the years that Robert Noble took it over in 1868 and really put it on the map.

My Father kept a one-line-a-day work diary most of his life and his entry for May 20TH, 1919 stated:

"W.J. Campbell took over the mill today. End of an era."
"Sic transit gloria mundi — so passes the glory of the world."

CHAPTER TWO
The Village

The fine old Maxted home, later Herb Caseley's, at the foot of Laird's hill – Johnnie, left, Hattie, their mother, and "Louie", circa 1895.

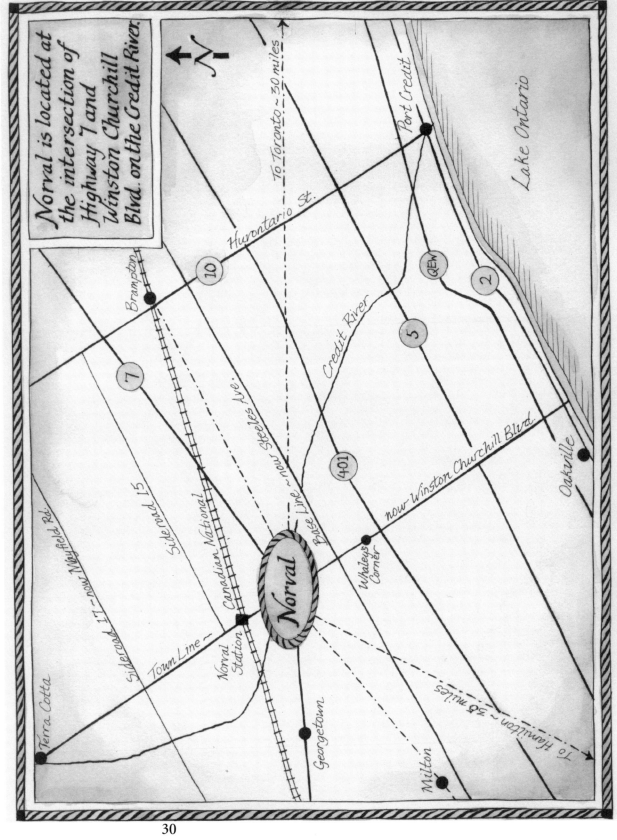

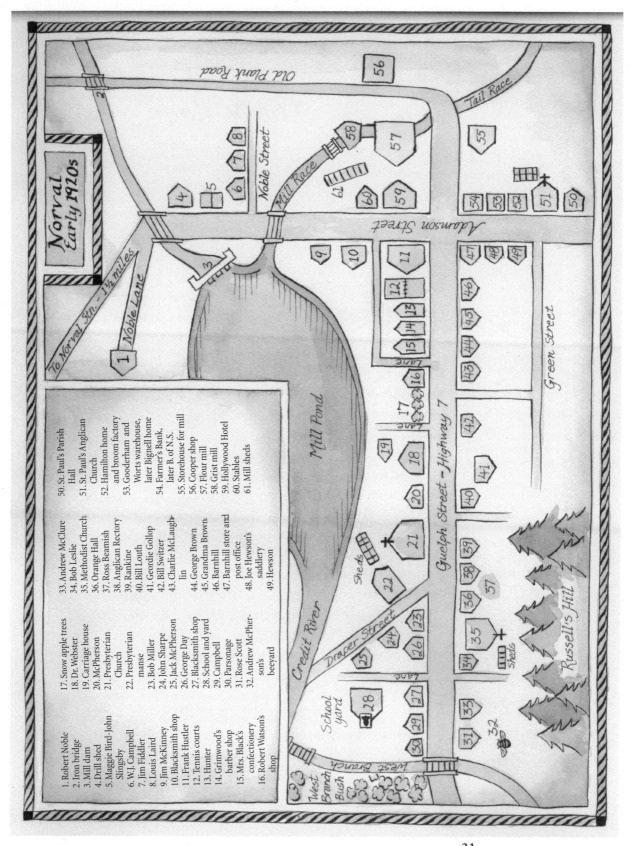

The Village

What has happened in and around the village of Norval is typical of so many small centres in Old Ontario. No more shoes for your horses, no beer on tap, no bank to hide your pennies, no hammer and nails handy, no home-ground flour for your bin, no butcher shop where Tom, the kindly old helper, would weigh out sausage and say "Now that's as close to three pounds as dammit is to swearing," no rubber boots and overalls on the store shelves, no haircuts for a quarter, no fragrant loaves from the baker firing up his woodstove oven, no resident doctor, and no glass fronted post office, where the mail came in twice a day. That was the place where the news in the old *Mail and Empire* took second place to the *real* news — the stuff that was happening on the home front, like who had died overnight, who had been born, or who needed help somewhere.

Building Highway 7 through the village started the big changes in Norval, as well as on surrounding farms. Trees and houses considered to be in the way were simply cut down or pushed over. Of the original five, there isn't a single iron bridge left in Norval; horses didn't like them because they rattled. Quiet country roads are a thing of the past; woe betide the cow that steps outside her fence and onto today's heavily traveled roads. Our earlier way of life has become a victim of progress.

But through all the changes, three structures have remained constant, the village churches — the Presbyterian, the Methodist (now the United Church), and St. Paul's Anglican. As some wit remarked back in 1925, the only thing wrong with Norval was that it had too many steeples and not enough smokestacks. We liked it the way it was.

Norval had so much to offer: a broom maker, two good saddlers, a carriage maker, shoe repairers, coopers to make your barrels, a bee-keeper for your sweet tooth and even a milliner. The farmers and gardeners looked to the village to sell their produce and grain, and businesses in the village depended on farm support for their income. There were two sawmills, two woollen mills and a brass foundry, all within village boundaries. At home we have part of a woollen sheet made in the 1870s by one of those mills; the sheets were light and warm.

Norval is located at the intersection of Highway 7 and Winston Churchill Boulevard, on the northeast edge of the County, in the heart of the Credit River Valley and surrounded by the everlasting hills.

A visitor to Norval in September of 1847 published an account of that visit in a Kingston newspaper, *The Whig Standard* and he was so impressed by what he saw that he wrote:

> "This exceedingly pretty Village is charmingly situated on a beautiful flat at one of the heads of the Credit. The Village is on one side of the stream, overlooked by majestic pines, on the other side a neat and commodious place of worship, surmounted by a glistening spire looking

Sam Curry's sawmill down river below the flour mill.

down on the Village like a Guardian Angel, while the beautiful river flows through the centre of the Village."

(CORRECTION: THE WRITER MISLOCATED THE
CREDIT RIVER AND ST. PAUL'S CHURCH SOMEWHAT.)

The visitor also added,

"I am astonished to find so much comfort, improvement and taste so far up in the backwoods. This Village contains five hundred inhabitants, has a post office, a grist mill with two runs of stones, a sawmill, a distillery, an oatmeal mill, two stores, a Church of England, a Presbyterian Church and two orange lodges."

Charles Unwin, Surveyor, wrote in 1853:

"The magnificent property purchased years earlier by James McNab, and situated halfway between York (Toronto) and Guelph, in the heart of the healthiest and most productive part of Canada, presents an opportunity of investment seldom to be met with."

Mr. Unwin was commissioned by General Sir Peter Adamson, the new owner of the McNab property, to lay out the land around Norval ("Esquesing Mills" as it was then called) into 500 lots. James McNab had envisioned a major industrial and residential metropolis, and Sir Peter tried to follow up that plan. However, he was slow in paying the survey crew and had to be sued for non-payment. In spite of this setback, Norval did develop into a thriving village and community and served a large surrounding area. An 1866–67 directory shows Norval as having two well-stocked nurseries, an extensive flax mill, two general stores, several churches, also a common school and a mechanics' institute. Also a branch of the Farmer's Bank, later replaced by the Bank of Nova Scotia. Gooderham and Worts, makers of whisky, had a distillery close to the mill race. There was also an ashery and a tannery nearby. The distillery's discarded mash was dumped in the Credit; it didn't occur to anyone to use it for cattle feed.

In 1926, Robert Leslie, living in the red brick house beside the United Church, could still remember his father hauling ashes to the tannery by oxen. He said this country was "redd up" (cleared) by oxen hauling good hardwood to be burned for the ashery, hardwood that would have cost a fortune in 1926. Robert also remembered the first time he heard a train whistle and it frightened him. The Leslie family had settled four miles from Norval in 1823 and Robert was the youngest of 10 children, all born without the presence of a doctor. His father would go with a yoke of oxen through the bush for a midwife. He also remembered the logging bees and the pig killings as great events. Whiskey was 20 cents a gallon!

Norval United Church – Bob Leslie's old home on the right.

In those early days, when people bought and sold by bartering, Mary Dawson Snider, a reporter for the *Toronto Evening Telegram* talked to an old lady who said she "had walked to Norval Village in her bare feet carrying a cured ham to trade for tea, when tea was a $1.00 a pound." She also traded butter and eggs for groceries, and remembered how her mother always had hams and dried apples hanging on hooks and racks in the farm kitchen. Her mother had also made a red and green plaid 'pinny' for her, which she loved to wear. "At the kitchen door," the old lady said, "we always had a big sugar kettle with dye in it for 'fullcloth' (serge) for father's clothes, which mother always made. We made our own candles too."

This interesting bit of family history came from Clarence Hunter, now of Chicago, who was one of the family of seven raised in Norval. Their mother died with lockjaw when they were quite young.

Alexander Ostrander and his wife arrived in Canada in the 1780s and took up land in the Niagara District. Within a year or two they harvested a crop of wheat. Up to that time they had depended on corn for flour, the corn being pulverized in a mortar, then put through a screen. The screen was made from an animal's pelt which had been thoroughly cleaned, then dried, stretched on a hoop and punctured with a hot spindle. The holes let the meal go through but held back the bran and chaff.

Wheat was a different problem. The sieve would not separate the bran from the flour. Mrs. Ostrander was determined to have a loaf of wheaten bread, so using her wits she thought of her Sunday bonnet lying useless in a trunk, got it out, ripped out the heavy lining, washed the bonnet, stretched it on a hoop, got a panful of pulverized wheat, and found the new sieve was just right. She soon had her wheaten bread and "shortcake" baking in the 'spider' over the fireplace coals. What a lovely treat! Despite the hardships of Mrs. Ostrander's life, she lived to be 104; she was born in 1752, died 1856. Younger generations of the Ostrander family subsequently came on to settle in Esquesing.

Norval Dam

The spider Mrs. Ostrander used was a deep three-legged iron pan which stood above the coals and hot ashes of the fireplace. Some years ago I recognized, and rescued, a spider in a garage sale.

The village lost some of its potential prosperity in 1856, when the Grand Trunk Railway by-passed it by a mile and a half. Colonel Alex Noble told me years ago that the railroad was originally planned to cross the valley just below the flour mill, but several landowners held out for more money so the railroad found themselves another route. Brampton and Georgetown profited but Norval lost out.

From the 1830s to the 1880s Norval did very well from the stage coach traffic. It was a favourite stopover between York (Toronto) and Guelph. The Hollywood Hotel, built in the early 1850s, had good stabling for horses and refreshments for travelers. Beer was five cents a generous glass.

In 1865 a petition was presented to the local council seeking permission to build the British American Hotel, and there were other accommodations in the locality, like the Dew Drop Inn in Centreville at the corner of Winston Churchill Boulevard and Embleton Road (or, as it was known for a hundred years the old Town line and #5 Sideroad).

Norval had a good band before 1900 and they practiced in the Orange Hall beside the Methodist Church, and also in the Drill-shed.

The Halton Rifles, later the Lorne Scots, met in the Drillshed across from the present Dam. The shed had been built in 1865 at the time of the Fenian Raid on Niagara (which didn't come to pass but had to be prepared for). The shed was taken down by Wes and Herb Louth in 1942, and rebuilt at Niagara-on-the-Lake to be used for target practice by the military during the 1939–1945 War.

In the 1920s one of the members of the famous Group of Seven artists discovered Norval and painted several canvases here. Granted, A.J. Casson took a little artistic license in his work and painted in a non-existent tree or two, but we knew exactly where he sat with his easel.

The first highway bridge over the mill race, 1921.

The Walk About in Norval Village

We'll start with the old iron bridge at the end of Noble's Lane, the bridge that carried us safely over the Credit River for one hundred years, but we must admit the new bridge of 1991 is a whole lot safer. When the old bridge was taken down the workmen said it was only by the Grace of God that a school bus hadn't gone into the whirlpool; the iron supports were rusted through.

The first house on the left is on the site of the Drillshed, where the Halton Rifles, later the Lorne Scots drilled in preparation to

Dr. Webster's home, later Prairie Maguire's, taken from Russell's hill when Norval had its trees. We called it "Maguire's Castle."

go to battle against the Fenians who were threatening Canada on the Niagara border. The community mustered forty men who actually spent six weeks on the Niagara frontier.

The next two buildings, Bill Pomeroy's home and the Credit Valley Boat Works and Canoe Country shop are built over John Slingsby's garden. John and his wife Polly (Bird) lived in the east half of the double house and Maggie Bird in the other half. Maggie's side had a grape arbour; it was nice to sit there in the shade. Peter Pomeroy now resides in John's old home.

Crossing over the mill race, now filled in to make parking space for the Hollywood Hotel, we come to the large red brick home of Nels Robinson, originally owned by Jim McKinney the blacksmith. His shop was just across the lawn. Behind the shop he kept a large pile of pine stumps, and when Jim had to put a steel rim on a wooden wagon wheel he would make a very hot fire in a confined space to heat and expand the metal rim. The pine stumps were virgin pine gathered from discarded local stump fences; they were full of resin and they burned like fury. When skaters on the mill pond wanted to have a fire on the ice Jim would lose some of his stumpwood.

The garage just ahead is Charlie Carney's, but was originally Frank Hustler's workshop, and the present carpet outlet was Frank's hardware store.

Turning up the street, the gas pumps on the corner are gone, and so are the tennis courts, now the site of Bill Hunter's attractive home. Beside it the nice old frame house built long before 1900 was the Hunter home of Bill's father and grandfather. Beside that again is the Dunlop home, unrecognizable from the original Grimwood Barber Shop. There is a new home on the lot where Mrs. Black's confectionery burned down and there you will find Jim Fiddler, (a great grandson of Joseph and Sara Bird) who has "come home" to live in Norval.

The Watson home, on the edge of the sidewalk, was built around 1850 and is now an antique shop. The Snow apple trees in the garden have been gone so long that hardly anyone remembers them being there. A little mall occupies their space now.

"Hope Cottage", Dr. Webster's lovely old home, has succumbed to commercial interests, and the carriage house at the back hasn't seen a horse since the first Great War.

Next, the McPherson home, "Inverholme", built in 1854 by Henry Gooderham, has lost it gardens to parking, as did Dr. Webster's place.

The impressive Presbyterian Church with its spacious grounds is still intact, complete with the manse where their ministers have resided since the church was built in 1878, the year my mother was born. The Reverend Ewan MacDonald and his wife, L.M. Montgomery, lived in the manse from 1926 to 1935.

On Draper Street we had Bob Miller on the corner, then John Sharpe, Justice of the Peace, and then "General" Jackson's wee shoe repair shop. The General's daughter, Minnie, married Jack McPherson from just around the corner.

The George Day residence across from the Methodist (United) Church is well into its second century, but there is no trace of the blacksmith shop; a used car concession occupies that space.

Our old school is long gone and its replacement, built in the 1960s, is now a daycare centre. Local school children are bussed in four different directions, and in the process lose their sense of community.

The L.M. Montgomery Garden is on a portion of the former school ground and the huge rock in it holds a dedication plaque to her. At the other end of the village is a park named in honour of James McNab. We hope other notable people like John Forster, Robert Noble and Sam Webster will be somehow honoured in the village as well.

The fine iron fence around the Presbyterian Church. The Anglican Rectory is across the road, and Russell's pines can be seen on the hill behind.

Beside the L.M. Montgomery Garden is a listed Heritage Home, formerly the Campbell's, and beside the West Branch of the Credit River is the former manse of the United Church.

Now, crossing the highway and reversing your steps, three old homes are gone, but Andrew McClure's frame home and Bob Leslie's brick home beside the United Church are well remembered.

The United (Methodist) Church has been a Rock of Salvation in the valley long before the congregation was established in the present brick building. When Church Union came about in 1925 between the Methodists, the Congregationalists, and some Presbyterians, the Rock was shaken but didn't go down. Neither did the Presbyterian Church, but it was a difficult time for many of the old families.

The Orange Lodge stood beside the Methodist Church and it was big enough to hold several hundred people at concerts and other social functions. It was burned down in 1972, having served as a garage for some years.

The Anglican Rectory, a tall brick house, was built in or around 1917–18, and was sold in the early 1960s.

The Dunlop Insurance business sits on the Rankine's lawn, and Bill Louth's home has been replaced by a photographer's shop.

Geordie Gollop's house is still there on the side of the hill but the fabulous tulip beds have disappeared, along with all the Gollops in the village. Just one Gollop is left in the broader area, Barbara, who married Al Ferri.

The George Brown home is next.

The fine three-generation Barnhill home is now a chiropractic clinic; next to it, Barnhill's store and post office now stand vacant.

Across from Barnhill's store is the old Bank of Nova Scotia building, now a hair salon.

Continuing along Adamson Street towards the cemetery hill, we pass the former butcher shop, next the site of the Gooderham and Worts Distillery warehouse (now Carter's

Geordie Gollop is in his element, showing his beautiful garden to visitors, early 1950s.

St. Paul's Anglican Church, built in 1846.

new home) and an old brick cottage which was owned by a Mr. Hamilton who operated a small broom factory. I can remember standing at the door of that tiny "factory" and watching Mr. Hamilton stringing the brooms. The place burned down in the 1920s and nearly took St. Paul's Anglican Church with it.

St. Paul's was built in 1845–46, but previous to that the congregation was served by circuit riders, as were most of the early settlements. One of the earliest saddle-bag ministers on record was the Rev'd Adam Elliot whose parish extended from Lake Ontario to Parry Sound. Some years ago we were given a brass case in which a small Bible or Prayer Book could be carried and there is a ring on it to hang the case on the saddle horn.

Going back to the four corners we pass the site of Joseph Hewson's saddlery shop.

Almost the final stop, right on the highway, is where the flour mill stood for a hundred years. The grist mill, the cooper shop, the storage building and the mill sheds are completely gone. When there was a concert in the Orange Hall in the winter, people would come in sleighs and cutters, tie up and blanket their horses in the mill shed and the church sheds. The warm blankets would come off the horses and be wrapped around the children for the ride home. Nearing the foot of Laird's hill were other great old families, the Maxteds, the Whitfields, the Knights, the Blackburns, the Wiggins, and the Wheatleys. Only three homes of the old-timers are left. The Maxted home has been owned by the Caseley family for many years. A laneway to homes in the valley is now named "Caseley Drive."

The Hollywood Hotel

The Hollywood Hotel in Norval has been a landmark since about 1854, but not always under that name. It was a coach stop on the old plank road between York (Toronto) and Guelph with good accommodation for both travelers and horses. The stables were on the present parking lot. While there doesn't seem to be an actual record of a name change, we have a copy of a petition that was circulated on behalf of the British American Hotel for a liquor license and signed by about thirty of the local residents. In view of the fact that the biggest hotel was the later Hollywood, we believe the British American was one and the same.

When the carriage trade gave way to the automobile the hotel rooms emptied and so did the stables. The barn disappeared in the 1930s.

In the 1920s Mr. Bignell had a little shop and a tea room in part of the hotel; there was also a small bakery and John Smith rented space there for a butcher shop. Mrs. Hewson owned the hotel at that time, and when she sold it in the early 1930s the new owner turned it into a beer parlor, which was like having a license to print money. Peel Country was dry; Norval was the nearest pub to Brampton and the hotel did a land-office trade.

In the early 1920s when highway #7 was pushing west, the hotel was an obstruction, but a solution was reached by slicing off half of the front of the building from the roof down. Without the long verandah and the balcony the hotel lost its exterior charm and character.

In 1993 fire practically destroyed the old hotel but at the time of writing it is being rebuilt for whatever purpose. Once before, in the 1920s fire had broken out in the kitchen of the hotel but a bucket bridgade carrying water from the mill race averted a total disaster.

Dr. Jim Bovaird, Veterinarian, had his first office beside the arable at the back of the Hollywood Hotel. A story has come to hand that one of the local farmers who knew the doctor very well decided to play a harmless little trick on him, saying that he "owed him one!" The farmer discussed his plan with some of the boys in the village, told them he was going to call the veterinarian late that night and ask him to come and see "a very sick cow," knowing that he wouldn't refuse. One of those lads passed the word to his friend, "Doc" Bovaird, so in anticipation of that call Dr. Bovaird busied himself in making a very large pot of strong tea, put some in a drenching bottle and the rest in a proper medicine bottle, then sat back and waited for the phone call. It came about 11:30 p.m. The doctor hitched up his horse and drove to the top of Laird's hill, where the farmer was waiting with a lantern, and out to the barn they went. The supposedly "very sick cow" was pointed out, the doctor examined her very carefully (found nothing of course) and then played a little game of his own. He said "your cow is sick all right but thank goodness I happen to have some of the best medicine available for her ailment." He gave the cow the contents of the drenching bottle right away, then handed the full medicine bottle to the farmer, telling him to make sure the cow got a cupful every hour throughout the night. The doctor said he was sorry he couldn't stay himself as he would like to make another call, but he promised he would come back first thing in the morning to make sure the cow's fever was down.

And then that young Doctor Bovaird went quietly home to bed and slept the sleep of the just!

Not too long after the miraculous recovery of that "sick cow" the doctor married the farmer's daughter, and they moved to London, Ontario, where Dr. Bovaird had a most successful career as a veterinarian, especially in his work with horses. He died at the age of 101.

Henry Pettigrew, warden; Jim Fiddler, warden; and Rev. T. G. Wallace, rector, St. Paul's Church, 1899.

John Slingsby and Maggie Bird

John came to Norval from Cumberland, England, as a very young man, and around 1890 he married Mary Elizabeth (Polly) Bird. They farmed for a short time just west of the village at the dead end of the 10th line. One of the fields on that farm was known as "Poverty's Peak"; nothing would grow on it. After his stint on the land, John worked in Noble's mill, grinding chop and other grains in the grist mill. He and Polly lived in the east half of the white double house directly across from the dam, and Maggie Bird lived with her mother in the other half. John had one Old Country expression that I remember; when children were misbehaving he didn't blame the youngsters, he would just say "Their broughtin's up are at fault."

Maggie Bird, also from Cumberland, was one of a family of seven who settled in the Norval area. She was a dear and gentle little soul who made her living sewing and taking in boarders, usually the school teachers. The board money was never over twenty dollars a month, possibly only fifteen dollars. When John's wife Polly, was sick, Maggie looked after her too. I can remember my mother taking me to see her when I was five. "Aunt" Polly reached across the bed and handed me a little pebbly brown teapot with lily-of-the-valley on the side. I wanted to have tea in it as soon as we got home but Mother said "wait till you are older," and I haven't made tea in it yet.

After Polly died, Maggie would make John a hot dinner, but before he came into the kitchen from working in the mill, she would sweep him down with her broom, for he would be covered with flour and mill dust. She was just tidy, not house-proud.

These two people, John Slingsby and Maggie Bird, seemed to symbolize a quality of life that people valued in those days — an old world courtesy, a great love for their church and all it stood for, and quiet contentment in their home. Am glad I knew them both.

Maggie Bird with her mother, Sara (Noble) Bird.

Mrs. Black's Confectionery

Mrs. Black's store was a magnet for every child who walked up that street. In retrospect, the shop window was probably no more than four feet across, but it held everything kids wished for — long licorice sticks, caramels, pink jelly shapes, and little paper bags with icing sugar in them which you sucked with a straw. There were clay marbles in all the rainbow colours, and glass alleys which you could seldom afford. On a great occasion you could buy ice cream and eat it at an iron table in Mrs. Black's own parlour. I made it there just once, for passing an exam. Mrs. Black also sold groceries.

Mrs. Black's father, Eli Gollop, and her brother had been saddlers, and one end of the rambling old home was the saddlery. The harness they made was of excellent quality and took many prizes at the fairs, which unfortunately caused some jealousy among other fair exhibitors. On one occasion, Eli, taking a last look around his shop the night before a big fair, discovered his beautiful new harness was cut through the leather in half a dozen places. He was very upset, but stayed up all night making another set, and won first prize anyway.

The confectionery burned down about 1944. Mrs. Black's sister-in-law, Mrs. Bob Gollop, was melting wax to cover jam when it overheated. And that was the end of that great little shop with the tinkling door bell; it tinkled you in and tinkled you out.

Aside from the personal losses in that fire, the saddlers' valuable collection of tools was destroyed.

The Village Blacksmiths

In our time there were just two blacksmiths in the village but in earlier days there were four in the locality and lots of work for them. The one we knew best was Jim McKinney's blacksmith shop, opposite the Hollywood Hotel stables. Mr. George Day's blacksmith shop

Blacksmith George Day's lovely daughters: Laura, Gertrude, Alice and Eva. He also had three sons, George Jr., Victor and Charlie.

Bill from Jim McKinney, 1922. Good work, well done, very reasonable prices!

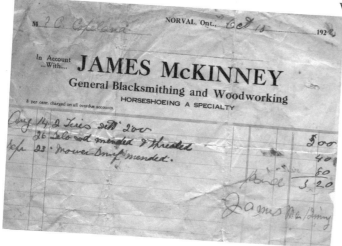

was just in front of the old Norval Public School. George had a family of seven, four girls and three boys, and lived in the big brick house across from the United Church. That home was a gathering place for my mother's generation. Play practices for the village and community Christmas concerts were often held there. George Day Jr. carried on the blacksmithing when his father had to retire.

Jim McKinney was a very rugged individual. I remember that his hands were gnarled and twisted and he was quite lame; his feet had been stepped on by too many horses, but he did try to be gentle with them. Some blacksmiths had a trick they used with a fractious horse; they pricked the animal's nose with a metal spring called a "twitch". They said it would take a horse's mind off his feet when he didn't like being shod!

We were often in McKinney's shop, the walls lined with horseshoes and foot-paring knives of all kinds. He showed us how a horse with ice shoes could keep his feet, with the cleats built at opposite angles to stop the slipping. The forge in the shop was red hot, and Jim's leather apron was covered with charred spots where sparks had landed. There was a special coal for forges and the forge was turned by hand. He always kept a pail of water beside the forge when using the anvil to shape or bend red-hot iron of any kind, for it had to be cooled quickly or it would lose its "temper."

Barnhill's General Store and Post Office

Three generations of the Barnhill family served the community well in the General Store and Post Office, situated on the west corner of the main intersection. When I was five years old I was trusted to go down to the store, over the two bridges, and fetch the Glendinning's daily paper, *The Mail and Empire* and on one of those trips Mr. Barnhill gave me a candy wrapped in gold paper. It was my first real chocolate. Many years later Hardy Barnhill did the same thing for our daughter. Nice to remember.

That store had everything you needed, from aspirins to bananas, overalls, boots and shoes and good cheeses which came in a big wheel. For many of us the Christmas decorations in that store window were all that we would see and we certainly kept an eye on them.

The Post Office, established in 1836 when the name McNabsville was changed to Norval, was across the back of the store, and the letter boxes reached almost to the ceiling. When the mail was being sorted, (it came in twice a day) a wee little door in front of the letter boxes would be closed. The rural mail carriers each had their own corner to sort the country mail. Both rural routes covered 12 to 15 miles on mud and gravel. Jack Mitchell, Jack Graham and his son Jack, Elsie Grimwood and Charlie Rankine all served the farmers well. I am not too sure about this but I think Charlie Rankine was the first carrier to use a car instead of a horse and buggy.

The mail came in by train to the old Grand Trunk station a

Hardy Barnhill at the door to the Post Office that ruled his life for many years – he was sorely missed when he left the village.

mile and a half north of the village; Lou Laird with his truck was the last of the carriers to meet the trains. Two of the earlier horse and buggy men were Jack Mitchell and Robert Glendinning. At night they carried a lantern which swung from an extended hook on the buggy top.

Strange items came into the Post Office sometimes, but this one left no doubt about its proper destination:

> *"Mr. Postmaster, if you please*
> *Deliver this letter at your ease*
> *To Norval Post Office where you'll meet*
> *Mr. Eli Gollop who sells meat.*
> *His eyes are small, his hair is neat,*
> *You'll know him by his great big feet!"*

The postmark on that letter was "Norval, 1882."

In 1851 Col. Clay, the first Postmaster, threw a party to celebrate the completion of the plank road to Norval; according to the Streetsville Review papers of the day the party lasted till dawn. Also at that time there is early mention of a toll gate located on or near Walter Bianchi's hill about a mile below Norval.

When Barnhill's was sold in 1956, and the Barnhill's name was no longer associated with the post office, some of the heart went

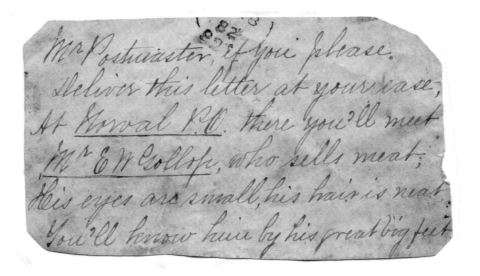

out of the village. The Post Office was really the core of the community, especially with the continuity of the Barnhill ownership, which lent a sense of stability in changing times.

To children the store was a treasure house. Under those wide counters were bins with glass fronts, and stuck on the glass were pictures of the fancy biscuits inside. We wished, oh how we wished; perhaps it was the pink icing that looked so good.

Sugar was six pounds for 25 cents, chocolate bars and Wrigley's gum were always a nickel, and Carhart's overalls about $3.00.

Before the telephone era people wrote a lot of letters, and it was a pleasure to pick up the mail every morning. But when war broke out in 1939, getting the mail took a different twist — with family members thousands of miles from home you never knew if the letter in your hand might well be the last one. Much of the mail was censored and read before it ever reached you.

Grandad driving old 'Mona' who carried mail twice a day from the Grand Trunk Railroad Station. The passengers are L. Warwick Noble, and Dr. Clark Noble, who assisted Drs. Banting and Best on the famous Insulin project.

Robert Watson

Robert Watson's home was very close to the sidewalk and his shop was the front room of the house. When #7 Highway was being constructed through the village, Mrs. Watson had a hard time keeping the dust down on the verandah, let alone in the house. Other women of the village complained, too, but the highway men just shrugged and the dust kept piling up. So one fine morning Mrs. Watson and Mrs. Campbell, at the upper end of the street, swept their porches, put the sweepings in jars, got on the old Radial to Toronto, went straight to Queen's Park and demanded to see the Premier, the Hon. Mr. Drury. They showed him the sealers full of dust and told him why they were upset, and asked him what he was going to do about it. The very next day the dust was being controlled.

Robert Watson's grandfather, William Watson, had taken over the little oven-shed behind the house. A Chinese baker was the first to use that oven. Mr. Watson Jr. was said to have made the finest bread you ever ate. And no doubt the flour came from Noble's Mill, just down the street. On Saturdays he often had to make a third batch of bread just to keep everybody happy.

From the earliest years of the Methodist Church, the Watson name had a prominent place in the church records.

When the custom bakeries started to deliver bread to Norval in the early 1920s, the home bakeoven was seldom used; it was too labor intensive. You could buy bread at the door for eight or 10 cents a loaf.

An advertisement for the Norval Post Office and General Store.

Hustler's Hardware

The only hardware store in the village at the turn of the century was owned by Mr. Soles, who was always referred to as "Daddy" Soles. Mr. Frank Hustler bought the store in 1913. Frank had the agency to sell Ford cars, and he also sharpened plough-shares, lawnmowers, cutting-box knives, etc. and did acetylene welding. However, despite all that work at home he always said his "survival income" came from field work in the farming area. He sold DeLaval milking machines, cream separators and steel stabling, installed bathrooms, and serviced practically everything he sold.

Before electric lights came to Norval about 1919, everyone

used kerosene for lamps and lanterns. Kerosene (coal oil) was 10 cents a gallon. Farmers would bring their empty 45-gallon drums back for refilling and stack them against the side of the store next to the Hollywood Hotel. The village boys would sit on them in the evenings and beat a tattoo with their heels on the empty drums as they chatted.

Mrs. Hustler had trouble sleeping with that nightly clatter going on under the bedroom window. So did her husband Frank, for two reasons: the racket, of course, in one ear, and also the suggestions he was hearing in his other ear. So, as Benjamin Franklin said so nicely two hundred years ago, "At the instigation of my wife whose wishes I find it inconvenient to thwart," Frank crawled out of bed, found a bucket, filled it with cold water, very quietly opened the bedroom window and tipped the bucket over the window sill. The drumming stopped abruptly. Silence reigned.

An advertisement for the Norval Meat Market

Every year in early spring Frank bought a railway carload of wire fencing for the farmers and often helped them "stretch" it. And every year, too, he bought four tons of binder twine for the farm grain and cornbinders, two very different implements. When straw balers appeared on the farms special wire was needed to tie up those straw bales. Baling twine came later.

As a young man of eighteen on the Hustler farm on the Tenth Line, Esquesing, Frank suffered a severe injury while cutting wood in the bush. His axe slipped and sliced the toes on one foot almost off. Some hours later when Dr. Webster got to him he just sewed the toes back on and Frank didn't lose any at all. It makes your back bone creep just to think about the pain he must have felt. Frank was the eldest of the family; his father had died, and his mother depended on Frank for the farm work and the chores.

Some time after buying the store Frank purchased a Model T 1913 Ford car with a brass radiator and acetylene headlamps and tail lights. There was a calcium carbide tank on the running board on the driver's side. By adding water to the calcium carbide you generated acetylene gas which was very unstable. Frank couldn't get the acetylene lamps to ignite so he kept adding more water, leaning over the tank and opening the top a little to let the water soak into the calcium carbide. It still wouldn't ignite — the system must have been plugged — but in the meantime a tremendous pressure had built up in the carbide tank. Suddenly it exploded right through the garage roof, peeling some skin off Frank's forehead as it went past. Had he leaned just a little farther over that tank, his head would have gone through the roof, too.

Frank also sold gas. There weren't too many cars around in 1920 but once the highway was finished the trade was good. Gasoline was 18 cents a gallon.

Frank was quick to respond in an emergency. While working at the mill as a carpenter, my dad had the misfortune to puncture his left hand when a screwdriver slipped. He went to Frank for a bandage, bleeding like a stuck pig. Frank took one look at that hand, grabbed a can of turpentine, said "Charlie, this is going to hurt" and then poured the turpentine through the hole. But it did clean the wound and slowed the bleeding. That was a sore touch; working men had to be tough in those days.

The Hustlers had two sons, Harland (who was killed on his motorcycle) and Lloyd, an engineer and a gifted organist. Harland had an inventive mind, and at age 14 built a steam engine and a crystal set radio which needed ear phones.

Mr. and Mrs. Hustler shared their car with many older people. In 1922 they took my Grandmother Glendinning for a drive. She wanted to try riding in a car but wondered if the contraption was safe!

The Orange Hall

A traveler passing through the village long years ago wrote that he "Had never before seen so many Orange Lodges in one small place." It is our conclusion that the traveler was in too many pubs before he counted the Lodges, as the history books still show only one such lodge in Norval at any time in the first 100 years of the village's existence and none since.

The Orange Hall was a large building beside the Methodist Church, and was used as a Community Hall for musical entertainments, Town Meetings and Band practice. The Drill-shed was also used for band practice.

The 1890s and the early 1900s were great years for plays. I remember my mother telling us about one called "The Spinster's Convention" and the following year they staged "The Spinster's Return". Every character required two people to play it, the theme being that everyone really wants to be different from what they are. A short, dark-haired girl wants to be a tall and willowy redhead, and so on, and by walking through a hand-turned mockup sausage machine, they were "transformed" on the spot. The blondes came out black-haired, the redheads were blonde and the audience, who knew them all at home, were hard put to recognize the changes. "The Spinster's Return" was their return to real life and they were glad to be back.

Those plays were highlights of the year, but the Christmas Concerts in the Orange Hall outshone everything. The Christmas tree reached to the ceiling and was lit with real candles. I shudder now to think what could have happened if it had caught fire. All the school children and pre-schoolers were crowded in the front seats; parents filled the chairs and any available standing room. Dr. Webster was usually the Chairman, and Santa Claus was no doubt himself. My gift off that tree when I was five years old was put there by Rosie Scott, the adopted

Ken Robinson and Bill Carney in the 1940s. Bill remembers Norval as a great place to grow up, the hills and the river supplied year-round pleasure.

child of Jim and Jennie Scott who lived on until she was 97. She had packed a carved wooden box with cookies and candy. At the end of the concert every child was given a red cheesecloth bag with a dozen candies and an orange. For some of the children that would be the only orange they would see all year.

When the Orange Lodge disbanded, in the 1920s, the Hall was sold to Ross Beamish, who used it for a garage and repair business. Later, Percy Donaldson carried on the business until the building burned in 1941. Somehow the United (former Methodist) Church and Percy's house were saved, but it was a fierce fire.

Egbert C. Reed, 1886–1957 – Artist and Author

Mr. Egbert C. Reed was born in Toronto and was a graduate of the Ontario College of Art. He was well known in advertising circles, and was also known for the quality of his many portraits of famous Canadians. He was commissioned by the Canadian Government to do a series of portraits of the Allied Generals of World War II including General Montgomery, General Alexander of Tunis, General Eisenhower and several others. For a radio series he was also commissioned to paint the Mayors of various small towns in Ontario.

Aside from his art, he was very interested in helping underprivileged boys get a better start in life. Working with the late T.P. Loblaw and the Kiwanis Club, Mr. Reed helped to organize the "K" clubs in Toronto and he also worked with the Big Brothers association. He was a member of the Arts and Letters Club.

Mr. Reed was very proud that he had had an opportunity to paint "Thunder Cloud", the last living survivor of the massacre at Little Big Horn, famous as Custer's last stand.

Egbert's wife was Marion Noble, daughter of Colonel Alexander Noble, of "The Elms", Norval. Bert painted many landscapes of his beloved Credit Valley home. Bert had four children, Prudence (Bond), King, Julian, now our local Member of Parliament, and Laurie, a geologist.

Mr. Reed died at Christmas, 1957.

The Village Churches

The Christian pioneers who built the three local churches "built better than they knew." There they gathered on Sundays to worship God in peace, and preach the faith once delivered to the saints.

The Presbyterian Church was built in 1878, (the year my mother was born) to replace an earlier frame building on the present Hillcrest Cemetery land. We understand that the impressive stone church was built by the Laird brothers and some of the stone work was done by John Maxted. The ceiling of the Presbyterian Church is particularly beautiful.

The first Methodist Church was built in 1854 when Henry Gooderham and Thomas Forster spearheaded a drive to build it.

There was also a Disciples Church on the 10th Line which was moved over to the town line and became the home of Mr. and Mrs. Robinson and their large family.

St. Paul's Anglican Church is the oldest original structure, built in 1845–1846 of pine.

The Christian faith was deeply rooted in the hearts and minds of the early settlers, and the descendants of those same families are still active in their churches today. To name just two among many, there are the McClures in the Presbyterian Church, and the Laidlaws in the United (Methodist) Church. The Watson men too, hold a prominent place in the early records of the Methodist congregation.

There is an interesting note in the Anglican Vestry meeting of 1858 where "We, the undersigned, declare ourselves to be the United Church of England and Ireland," now the Anglican Church of Canada.

At St. Paul's, between resident Rectors, Divinity students would fill in for the services, and one of them, the Rev'd Russell Smith, wrote about his trips to Norval: "Like all the other students

Walter Brain, June 1935, donated lumber to build St. Paul's Parish Hall.

going out to Norval I used to stay with Mrs. Collins who lived beside the cemetery. She was an Anglican of the old school, glad to offer hospitality to everyone, especially the clergy. She had two beds, one for students and one for a Bishop and students were not allowed to sleep in the Bishop's bed. I can recall many a bitterly cold winter morning being wakened in the darkness at 5 a.m. by Mrs. Collin's musical alarm clock playing "Home Sweet Home" and me with the prospect of a two-mile walk through the snow to catch the 7 a.m. train at Norval Station."

The old Anglican Vestry notes reveal the names of many men in public life in the village: Sir Peter Adamson, who gave the land on which the Church was built, Colonel Clay, the first Postmaster in 1836, and the Pettigrew men. As a boy, Henry Pettigrew helped in carrying stones to build the foundation of the church.

The Baptismal Font in St. Paul's was dedicated as a Memorial to Mima Collins, who taught Sunday School there for years.

The Rev'd R.S. Boyd, Rector in the late 1920s, kept a goat in the little Rectory stable. The goat visited all the neighbors so often that she wore out her welcome. Mr. Boyd called the goat "Misery," as in "misery likes company." He finally, regretfully, had to part with her.

In the late 1940s and all through the 1950s, under the guidance of the Rev'd Jim Maxwell, extensive renovations were made in St. Paul's. A proper basement and a new furnace went in, a new chimney was built by Bud Carter, the stucco was renewed by the men of the church, the interior and exterior were painted, the ceiling was lowered, the old vestry was removed to the basement, the altar rail was rebuilt and a hardwood floor was laid in the chancel. An electronic organ replaced the old pump organ, and a cross was erected on the church steeple by Warwick Coupland.

In 1925 the Vestry of St. Paul's discussed the need for working space and for other events in the life of the church. A Parish Hall would fill that need. Mr. Walter Brain said he would donate the lumber, (which was standing in Walter's bush!) and C.W. Coupland agreed to head the building committee. The money for the building was raised within the congregation, and the building was almost totally erected by the men of St. Paul's. The work involved was considerable; just getting the logs in the bush cut and hauled to Archie Fuller's sawmill on the fourth line, Chinguacousy, all by team, took about a month. However, in 1927, the lumber was ready, the foundations had been well and truly laid, the erection of the building had proceeded, and in January, 1928, St. Paul's Parish Hall was dedicated by Archdeacon Scovil of Guelph, the Rev'd R.S. Boyd, Rector, and his guest, the Rev'd Neil McKinnon of Norval United Church. This year, 1997, marks the 70TH Anniversary of the completion of the Parish Hall. Dr. and Mrs. Webster donated the piano and the beautiful scenery for the back of the stage.

The Church Parish Hall has played the part of a Community Hall ever since it was built, serving as the location for so many good times, concerts, dances, plays, parties, receptions, all kinds of church activities, bazaars, meetings, Sunday School projects, church sponsored youth groups, Scouts, Guides and Young Peoples' Associations. The hall filled a vital need for St. Paul's and was of great benefit to the community. May it long continue to serve its good purpose.

St. Paul's W. A. pictured with the Rector, Reverend Dr. Grassett Smith. Included are: Bertha and Maggie Pettigrew; Sara Glendinning; Edith Rankine, Grannie Williams, Ida Hewson, Mrs. Robinson, Eva Day and Hilda Rankine.

CHAPTER THREE
Growing Up in Norval

Children playing outside the Norval school house, 1926/27

Growing Up in Norval

THE WALK TO SCHOOL

We had such a pleasant walk to Norval school in the 1920s. There was so much to see and do when we were six or eight years old that the three-quarters of a mile walk was just right. We checked out the wild pear tree on the hill and the sandpipers in the shallows between the dam and the iron bridge at the end of Noble's lane. We threw a rock in the whirlpool just to hear the thunk that told us the water was DEEP, then went on to the old apple tree just this side of the drillshed. I wish we had grafted some off of it before it died; those apples were so good. Next we went to see if the water level in the mill race was up or down. If it was too high the miller would open the huge gates at the dam, and if it was too low the brackets would have to go up on the apron of the dam to hold some water back. We made a stop at Jim McKinney's blacksmith shop to see if the horse he was trying to put shoes on was going to let him do it, and we liked to listen to him hammering on his anvil when he was using his forge. Then we went around Hustler's corner by the gas pumps, past the empty tennis courts, (too early though for tennis players) and on to Mrs. Black's window to see if there was anything new in the candy boxes, just in case we needed to know. Then we passed the picket fence across the front of Watson's garden, hoping some Snow apples had fallen outside the fence. Mrs. Doctor Webster had roses along the edge of her garden. After smelling the roses we came to Andrew Mcpherson's honey house; new honey smells great too. Bob Miller on the corner of Draper Street had red chickens. Sometimes they were out and we used to wonder if they laid red eggs; our chickens at home were black and white and they laid brown eggs. George Day's blacksmith shop was right in front of the school and if the school windows were open we could hear him working on his anvil too. Funny thing, when it was raining I don't ever remember wearing a raincoat to school. Maybe we didn't have any. If we ever complained about getting wet my little grandmother would say "you're neither sugar nor salt, honey, and you'll not melt."

On the way home from school one afternoon, walking past the drillshed, we spied some pennies on a low fence post, evidently left there by picnickers, along with their rubbish. We counted seven pennies; such wealth! That meant three each apiece, for who could need any more than that? We decided to throw the left over penny in the river. We stood on the bridge and tossed it in the whirlpool, and the current carried it a little distance downstream, like a skipped stone. A childhood moment I still remember.

The next day Mrs. Black did a roaring trade in licorice sticks, caramels and jelly beans!

A class photograph, 1920 – teacher, Miss Owens, presides. The author is pictured second row, fourth from left.

School Days

"School days, school days, dear old Golden Rule days, Readin' and Writin' and Arithmetic. All taught to the tune of a hickory stick!"

That was the case in 1920 when pupils had to pay attention when the teacher spoke to them. Norval's two room public school, school sections #7 and #27, straddling the township line of Esquesing and Chinguacousy, was built in the 1830s. On the wall in the senior room was a large picture of Queen Victoria, a landscape of a row of trees in France and a calendar from the Noble Flour Mill. There were five windows on the west side of the room, too high to see out of when you were sitting down, but not so high that we couldn't watch those big black cluster flies trying to climb up the window panes and falling over one another.

Arithmetic was the real stuff, the twelve times table was a must-learn chore; no such thing as adding machines in any school room. Our "hickory stick" was a black strap that was always kept in the teacher's desk and was used when you talked back, or if you were caught bullying kids on the playground.

Classes started at 9.00 a.m. with the Lord's Prayer, O Canada, or The Maple Leaf Forever. A 15 minute recess at 10:30, dinner hour 12:00 to 1:00, recess at 2:30, and home at 4:00.

All the country kids brought their noon meal and a lot of trading went on, like an apple for a cookie. Some of the pupils walked two and three miles twice a day, in all kinds of weather. When Red Craig Reid on the Georgetown road, #7 highway, was six years old and ready to start school he should have gone to Stewarttown, as their farm was in that school section. But that spring the bridge over the West Branch of the Credit River had washed out in a flood. His father contacted the Georgetown school board and asked if Craig would attend there. "Yes," they told him, "at $4 per month." Said Craig's father, "$4 for the family?" "Oh no, they replied, "$4 for each one that comes." Then his father said to Craig, "You'll walk to Norval." A long hike for a six-year old. Others came in from the ninth line, the tenth line, the

A picnic under the willows on the banks of the Credit River, 1937. Joan (Browne) Carter, Shirley Hargreaves, Bill Pomeroy and Owen Hughes – all grandparents today.

townline, the Ashgrove sideroad, (all of Esquesing) and from the fourth and fifth lines of Chinguacousy. Perhaps it was the long walk to school that gave Craig time to dream up mischievous pranks. In 1924 at age eight, Craig was left with his Grandfather Reid while his mother and dad went into Georgetown. Grandfather was sound asleep on the old couch in the kitchen. The coast was clear. Craig got into some firecrackers and set one off in the kitchen. He didn't get past the first one when Grandfather erupted off the couch and Craig headed for the barn. When Craig's parents turned up Grandfather said to them, "The trouble with you young people these days is you just don't know how to raise kids!" Nothing ever really changes. Grandfather must have seen the funny side of that caper, for when he could no longer drive, it was to Craig that he gave his prize horse.

In winter we wore overstockings and long underwear. The long wool stockings went on over our shoes, and a pair of rubbers went on over that again. The whole thing was a wretched nuisance.

Without a doubt we had one of the best playgrounds in the province: about two acres of flat ground for baseball and football,

Skating on our own pond – Roy, Warwick, Dick van Vliet, Ernie Driver and Bill Pierson in an early freeze-up, November 1933.

lots of trees around, the West Branch of the Credit beside the playing field and the "big river", as we called the Credit River, just over the fence. Russell's hill just across the road (#7 highway wasn't so busy in the 1920s).

Winter was great. We skated for weeks, often on rubbery ice, down on the pond, or we sleighed and slid on Russell's hill. That hill with its famous pines has given years of pleasure to several generations. L.M. Montgomery's writing room faced those pines. She was delighted with them. On Saturdays we took our sleighs to the hills on the roads, and when farmers brought grain to the mill to be ground into chop we hitched a ride up the hill with our sleighs at the end of a rope. Then we coasted back down and got another ride up the hill. We called this getting a "hookey."

When the teachers knew we were out on the hills or on the river at noon hour, they would ring a warning bell at five minutes to 1:00, which gave us *almost* enough time for another bobsled ride among the pines. The bobsled held six or eight of us. It was actually two sleighs joined by a plank that was bolted to each sleigh. We went like the wind right down to the gate behind Bob

Leslie's house, skipped over the highway and ran to the pump for a drink, (everybody drank out of the same dipper which hung on the spout). Then we found a nail to hang up our coats and made a mad dash for our desks. But if you had to make a detour to the two-holer out back you would be late for sure and have to write out a hundred lines like "I must not be late again" or whatever. In the early days, Eaton's and Simpson's catalogues, hung on a nail with binder twine, were the "toilet tissues." In the summer we had to contend with hornets; they seemed to like those little houses with a half moon cut in the door.

The hookey business almost got Dorothy Watson into deep trouble when she was ten years old. She had hookied herself and her sleigh to the top of the cemetery hill and was waiting for a clear track down then she saw the Broome girls from the tenth line coming along in their high old Model T Ford. Dorothy waited until they were well down the hill and then took off. However, the Broome girls drove very sedately in their horseless carriage and when Dorothy caught up to them at the foot of the hill she couldn't stop, so just flattened herself on the low sled, went under the car, shot out in front and headed for home. The Broome sisters and several men on the corner were shaken by what they had seen happening, but Dorothy was fine.

Andrew McPherson had a bee-yard just across the road from the school. On a mild February morning about 1924, the worker bees kicked out the drones, whose only function in life was to escort the Queen bee on her rounds. The drones flew across to the school yard, became chilled and comatose and ended up lying on the snow. Some of the boys recognized an opportunity, gathered up the bees in their mitts and after recess put the mitts under the coke burning pot-bellied stove to dry, as usual. The bees appreciated the warmth, crawled out of the mitts and flew happily about. Well, that was a day. The culprits had to confess or risk being expelled, which was the ultimate disgrace. For punishment they had to write 200 lines. The strap would have been a lot easier to take. My brother Warwick, along with Mac Watson, Clary Hunter, Jack Murray, Geordie Inglis, Terry Evans and Arnott Noble, spent hours writing out:

TO WALK A COUNTRY MILE

> *"How doth the busy little bee*
> *Improve the shining hours?*
> *On days that are sunny*
> *He is making his honey,*
> *On days that are cloudy*
> *He is making his wax.*
> *Bees don't care about the snow*
> *And I can tell you why that's so —*
> *Once I caught a little bee*
> *And he was much too warm for me."*

"Rigged" competitions in the larger regional fair prompted local trustees to set up the first independent Norval School Fair in 1926.

At that point no one seemed to know, or remember, that drones cannot sting.

Arbour Day in early May was a special occasion. We cleaned up the school yard, planted trees, took our lunches to picnic in the West Branch bush and then had a paper chase. The older boys were given bags of paper clippings and a head start of fifteen minutes, and the rest of us had to follow their paper trail, hoping to anticipate their game plan and catch them before the finish line, which was always back at the school.

In September we had the School Fair. Next to the Christmas concert it was the great event of the year. Previous to 1924–25, the Fairs had included a number of schools: Ashgrove, Stewarttown, Limehouse Quatre Bras, Ligney, Bannockburn and Norval. The Fairs were held in the biggest school, usually Georgetown. Our local trustees, Bob Murray, Harry Hunter, George Brown, Charlie Coupland and Bert Snow decided that the system was unwieldy and awkward, and worse, that the competition was often "rigged." The last straw in their decision to have their own Fair was when they saw a filled, iced, and decorated three-layer cake, made by a nine year old take first prize, when that class called for a plain white cake in a square pan with no icing. The rules had been

---

NORVAL SCHOOL FAIR

Splendid Success — Large Exhibit — Good Attendance.

Something new in School Fairs, started last year, was carried out again this year at Norval's second annual school fair. The baking was done under supervision at the school on the morning of the fair. The sewing and darning was also done with the judges present. The art work, writing, maps, etc., had been previously done under supervision of the teachers, and the vegetables and flowers grown from seeds supplied by the Board.

When the exhibit was ready at 10.30 a.m. there was a fine display in all lines. Mrs. Kennedy and Mrs. O'Neill of Georgetown, and Mr. A. McClure and Mr. Morganson of Norval, made excellent judges. Lunch was served at noon by the ladies of the Women's Institute and consisted of sandwiches, cake and coffee.

A booth on the grounds provided refreshments, the proceeds of which go into a fund for the 1927 fair.

changed on the spot. That winter Norval school committee held euchre parties in the school to raise money to buy garden seeds which were distributed to the pupils in April, four packages each, their own choice, two of flowers, two vegetables. The pupils could exhibit only what they had grown themselves.

Under guidance, the boys made milk stools and bird houses. On the morning of the Fair the girls baked tea biscuits and muffins. Coal oil stoves were brought in, with ovens, and you waited your turn to do your thing. When I was ten my dad made me a bakeboard from a single piece of white pine; it is still in regular use and I treasure it. The Fairs were a real learning process in a fun setting. The school walls were covered with collections of leaves, weeds, compositions and art work; the vegetables and flowers were set up on plank tables. The dog show outside was something else. A motley crew turned up. One 7-year old, who would tell you his name was Lornie Archie-baldheaded- Wardlaw, brought his ornery pup, who would neither sit, stand or walk at any command. He simply laid down, and sadly didn't get a prize. Said Lornie, "You're just a mut dog, you didn't even get me a nickel for an ice cream cone." But a kind soul watching cheered him up with five cents for his pocket.

Then there was the annual Christmas concert. No matter what was done or not done on that stage the parents and friends clapped with enthusiasm. One recitation I remember was Stewart Macdonald reciting half a dozen verses his mother, L.M. Montgomery had written for him. The last line of every verse was "and Stewart gets the neck." Apparently, once when they had company at the Manse and chicken was on the menu, Stewart came up short. At that same concert, Marie Laird and Jimmie Brown, aged eight and nine, sang a duet. "Where are going my pretty maid?" he sang. "I'm going to milk my cow" she said, swinging a milk pail and wearing a pretty blue gingham dress. The verses have escaped me but it

> Mac Watson; petunias, Milly Caseley; zinnias, Dorothy Watson; larkspur, Lee Watson, Martha Murray, Mary Copeland; everlasting, Lee Watson; mixed bouquet, Marie Smellie, Dorothy Watson.
> Domestic Science—Biscuits, Mary Copeland, Dorothy Watson; muffins, Mary Copeland; light cake, Dorothy Watson; dark cake, Dorothy Watson; collections of leaves (senior), Mary Copeland, Marie Smellie, Jimmie Harvey, Jack Murray; junior, Sarah Mackie, Marie Laird, Fursy Harvey, Jimmie Brown.
> Writing—Primer, Franklin Cleanes, Bruce Reid, John Hunter; Part One, Douglas Rankin, Joe Harvey, Weir Reid, Marie Laird; Two Class, John Mackie, Sarah Mackie, Jack Wardlaw, Evelyn Graham; Three Class, Herbie Roshier, Marie Smellie, Dick Graham, Isabel Wardlaw; Four Class, Dorothy Watson, Geo. Biguell, Elgie Varey, Mary Copeland; drawing, pencil drawing, Dorothy Watson, Mac Watson, Mary Copeland; design, Marie Smellie, Dan Murray, Joy Laird, Horace Biguell; collections of art, Four Class, Dorothy Watson, Stewart MacDonald, Mary Coupland, Geo. Biguell; Three

Seeds were distributed; pupils could only exhibit what they had grown themselves.

was a real hit. Only a year or so later Jimmie and his two sisters were all killed by the Radial at the top of the Cemetery hill.

For many years Charlie Williams, the school caretaker, looked after the stoves, cleaned the floors and kept a kindly eye on all of us. On one occasion Joe Harris, the Principal, had to reprimand one of the boys for coming into class with his boots covered in red clay. Said Joe "You will stay after four and wash the floor; it not fair to Mr. Willaims to have to clean up that mess." After school that day when the lad was down on his knees with a bucket of soap and water, his father came in looking for him, saw what he was doing and said to the teacher "We pay a caretaker to do this, the boy shouldn't have to do it." The teacher replied "That boy is staying here until he finishes that job." He told the parent why. The parent understood and waited quietly for his son.

About 1925 the trustees felt that we should have something hot with our sandwich dinners, so a very small kitchen was walled off in a corner and a four-burner coal oil stove was brought in, as well as assorted cups, plates and cutlery. We took turns helping prepare the boiled potatoes, cabbage and cocoa. We enjoyed our boiled potatoes and our cocoa.

Playground equipment was simple in the extreme: a baseball and bat, a football and one swing. We had our own skipping ropes, our own marbles and our own "jacks," with which we played a game with a small ball. Skipping songs varied from one community to another. Most of them I forget, but this one stayed with me:

> "Nev-er - skip-on - a-lit - tle-crack
> Or-you - will-break - your-Mo - ther's-back,
> If-you - skip-on - a-lit - tle-stone
> Your-dog - will-nev - er-get - a-bone,
> If-you - skip-on - your-sis - ter's-toes
> She-might - just-bop - you-on - your-nose!"

Skipping rhymes never needed to make any sense or be explained to anybody, they just happened. A. A. Milne would have understood perfectly.

Cooking up some corn on the banks of the Credit River, 1938 – Clark Lyons, Dick van Vliet, "Little" Bud Carter and Duncan Robinson.

We had some great teachers in the 1920s; Miss Owens and Miss Kate McColman in the Junior room, and Miss Beatrice Maxwell and Mr. Harry Peel in the Senior room. The teachers boarded in local homes at $4.00 to $5.00 a week and their salaries ranged from $500.00, maybe $600.00 a year, up to $900.00 for the Principal.

The school Inspector came at least once a year, and for reasons we didn't understand then, the teachers seemed to be in a state of apprehension. Mr. Deneyes, the Inspector was quite lame, had a booming voice, carried a cane and would appear bright and early in the morning. We all had to stand up and say in unison "Good Morning, Mr. Deneyes" and then we'd sweat out the rest of the day trying to appear invisible. Nobody wanted to be the one called up to the front of the class to spell what the Inspector would refer to as a word in everyday use, like ambiguous, Saskatchewan, or magnanimous. At a time like that your own inherent perspicacity goes right out the window. The Inspector had to make sure the teacher was keeping proper records of attendance and that she was covering the required work. The Inspector could make or break a teacher; his recommendation was vital to her success if she chose to move on. No wonder we were always warned to behave.

In the 1920s and 1930s some of the rural, one-room school boards could be more than a bit demanding when it came to hiring a new teacher. The salaries were pitiful. An 85-year old ex-teacher told us she taught 59 pupils, in a more isolated area, and her wages were $350 a year. That was in 1934. And from another ex-teacher came this partial list of "Rules for Teachers": "They could not marry during the term of their contract, could not go out after 8:00 p.m., could not ride in a carriage or a car with any man unless he was their father or a brother, could not smoke, could not wear bright colours, or dye their hair, and must wear at least two petticoats, never shorter than two inches above their ankle."

The job also required that the teacher must keep the schoolroom clean, sweep the floor every day, and scrub the floor once a week, clean the blackboards, and start the fire in the schoolroom at 7:00 a.m. so the room would be warm by 8:00 a.m.

This is an example of the terms in a contract that a teacher was asked to sign.

One thing for sure about our public schooling in Norval — when we left the Entrance class behind us and went on to High School, we knew how to add, subtract, and multiply, could read intelligently, knew something of grammar and could spell without too much difficulty. Canadian history had opened a door into our past, and in geography we learned where the world was; we had pinned it down a hundred times and we left it in good shape. That was June, 1927, and I was twelve and a half.

Teen Years

The teen years of course were our High School years. Just getting to school was often difficult. We had to go by train. When weather was particularly bad, my brother Warwick would meet the night train (7:00 p.m.) with the horse and buggy. The horse, old Jenny, didn't like trains, and one night when the engineer let some steam off at the station, Jenny, with three of us in the buggy, charged for the station yard gate, demolished part of it, dumped us out over a deep ditch and took off for home. The engineer, watching all this, stopped at the crossing, prepared to put us in the baggage car and head for Guelph Hospital. When he saw we were all mobile he carried on, but there was real concern at home when Jenny appeared, her harness trailing and no buggy in sight.

Money in the 1930s was as like hen's teeth; there wasn't any. So you mostly made your own fun. However, going to the theatre for an evening was 50 cents. A dance in the Parish Hall in Norval was also 50 cents, but there was a generous supper at midnight. Orchestras playing for the dances included "The Century Boys" from Toronto, Andy Frank's "Sodbusters" and Dorin Hull's group from Stewarttown. The Turkey Supper at the Presbyterian Church needed another 50 cents and the tables would be laden with the best of country cooking. Their Garden Party was 25 cents, ice cream 5 cents and a large piece of pie 10 or 15 cents. Stawberry

Some members of the Sunday picnic gang in the mid 1930s.

Socials were 25 to 35 cents with plenty of cake and real cream.

One of our greatest pleasures in our teen years was a picnic. Early Sunday afternoon we would gather up the local farm kids, boys who had come over from Scotland, Ireland and England to work on Canadian farms, and head up the Credit River. We would have four or five pounds of round steak at two pounds for 25 cents, a bottle of ketchup, 20 cents, several loaves of bread at 12 cents a loaf, a biscuit pan cake from home, milk and coffee. So for less than $1.00 in cash outlay, at least eight of us had a 2 o'clock dinner. We had made a fireplace on a sandbar about a mile up the river. Our grill was the concave out of an old threshing machine found in a farm dump, and our saucepan and coffee pot hung on a broken limb. All very primitive but adequate. Good drinking water was no problem. We had noticed a damp patch on a nearby bank, so we broke the bottom out of a ketchup bottle, stuck the broken end in the bank and in a few minutes we had water on tap. It made excellent coffee boiled in the embers and to settle the grounds we threw in a handful of clean sand.

That water and sand *must* have been clean as several of the gang were still around in their eighties!

Sometimes we made fudge over that fireplace, and to cool it we floated it in a pan downstream. On occasion the pan was intercepted and "liberated" but there was always plenty for everyone. If we caught any fish we would wrap them in blue clay, bury them in the hot ashes for 10 minutes, then peel both clay and skin off and enjoy the nice white meat. After we had washed up the dishes, in the river of course, we would spend a couple of hours searching for arrowheads in a nearby field, where there had once been an Indian encampment. We would find lots of flint, some arrow pints, once a spear head, a skinner or two, and bits of pottery and the odd wampum bone bead. We could never stay long enough to have an evening campfire and watch the moon come up over the river because for farm kids there were always the chores: bringing the cows in from the pasture for milking and taking the milk cans to the cooling tank. That routine never varied. Chores were just a way of life.

We did enjoy those picnics — no coolers, no pop, no ice

cream, just the walk and the river and the good companionship. It didn't matter if the meat was scorched at times, we just covered it with ketchup and ate it as a sandwich. And when we fanned out across the field to look for arrowheads, there was always the pleasant thought in your mind that a ghostly little Indian might be tracing your own footsteps as you picked up the chips of flint. The day I found the spearhead there was a fine little blue feather beside it. Coincidence? Or perhaps a little gift?

At times we would leave off arrowhead hunting and walk a mile farther up the river to The Dynamo, the first electrical power plant to transmit power in North America. It was still functioning in the 1930s and provided power for the Barber paper mill in Georgetown. Later in the 1930s it was practically destroyed by heavy floods but we could still walk along the beams and poke around the timbers. Building that dynamo was really a remarkable achievement by our Canadian engineers; Henry Grimwood from the village was the night watchman for the Dynamo.

In those years the radio was a marvelous source of entertainment. If, having had supper at 5:00 p.m., we could finish the evening chores by 7:00 p.m., (milking, feeding and bedding down all the animals in the stables) we came in, washed up and listened to "Amos and Andy." The Castrol Hour was splendid music, the Melody Boys from London, Ontario provided a lot of comedy, and there was also Don Messer and his "Islanders", George Wade and his "Cornhuskers", and Toronto's Royal York Hotel Orchestra with Luigi Romanelli. The big bands of the 20s and 30s all had good singers: Rudy Valle, Guy Lombardo and his wonderful, unforgettable 'Royal Canadians' and Mart Kenny's band.

My brother Bob had built a small crystal set radio which was hard to hear, so Dad in 1926 got a battery radio from Frank Hustler, and it was paid for by supplying the Hustlers with two quarts of milk every day for one year. We carried the milk down during the week but Lloyd Hustler came up the hill for it on weekends. We tried to use the radio sparingly, at noon for the weather and brief news, and perhaps two hours in the evening. We couldn't get hydro on our road until 1936, so our radio had to be run off a battery which had to be charged frequently. Mother loved the Christmas music so we tried to curtail our listening in December so the battery would hold up for Christmas.

The rural telephone system, with headquarters in Snelgrove, was weird and wonderful. Your "line" might have a dozen or fifteen subscribers on it. You listened for your own ring. Ours was one long and one short: 1 – 1. And then there was 1 – 2, 1 – 3, 1 – 4, 1 – 5. Then reversed as 2 – 1, two long and one short, 2 – 3, 2 – 4, and so on. We have a 1920s telephone book which covers most of Southern Ontario, and it is a slim book, too. A private conversation was not necessarily as private as one might think. It wasn't that neighbors listened in a harmful way; it was more like a social contact, but you weren't always aware it had taken place!

Hallowe'en hi-jinks in the 1920s and 1930s didn't raise too many eyebrows. A gate would go missing, a picket fence might change colour overnight or someone's House of Parliament (privy) was set up on the highway in the middle of the four corners and labeled "Office of the Ministry of Transport," or any other organization the young people wanted to honour.

This Hallowe'en yarn I heard from an old farmer years ago. Apparently a landowner in the neighborhood had got off on the wrong foot with several local boys, so one year the gang got a very long ladder and, working with long ropes, they hauled a farm wagon onto the barn roof straddling the ridge and then loaded it with bags of grain. The farmer was flabbergasted the next morning. How could he ever get it down? A couple of days later he had two visitors, who were so surprised at what they saw on the roof, they offered to find a crew who would lower the wagon and put the grain back in the granary. Which they did, ending in a nice way what could have been a festering grudge. The landowner had been paid in full; he had had two days of anxiety, and time to rethink his relationship with the neighbors. He was now obligated to them. The old farm dog was smart. He never said a word, just wagged his tail.

In the 1930s many young people came out from Britain to work on Canadian farms. They were almost all from cities or towns and their knowledge of farm ways and farm work was practically nil. But most of them were willing to learn and make good

Some of the Sunday walkers in the mid-1930s – Roy, Warwick, Gladys Linham, Dr. Ethel Noble, Bill Pierson and Ernie Driver.

in a strange country. But there was the odd one who let us know we were just colonials and as such not much could be expected of us. My mother used to gather up some of those boys on a Sunday after Church, for she felt sorry for them so far from their homes. However, one of them was a bit hard to take. He would mention that his farmer boss got him out of bed in the middle of the night (5:00 a.m.!) to go to the barn, no one brought him tea at 4:00 p.m. and he had to do chores on Sundays. (What else was new?) Anyway, one Sunday afternoon when six of us were sitting on the back porch we asked him if he had ever done any shooting. "Of course" he said, so we brought out a 12-gauge shot gun and shells, a .22 rifle, and an 1865 muzzle loader, complete with shot, powder, wadding and a ramrod. The boys loaded the muzzle loader *very* lightly, and one of them shot a tin can off the post. Then another lad, with the same light load in the gun, hit another tin can, after which that heavy weapon was reloaded and offered to our guest, with a warning that it had a kick like a mule. He had watched the others firing it without any obvious difficulty so he confidently shouldered the gun, pulled the trigger, and went stumbling back until a solid wall brought him to an abrupt stop.

The colonials had put a double charge in that gun!

CHAPTER FOUR
The Depression Years

1930 Oldsmobile Coach
CASH PAYMENT **$150.00** Balance Arranged

'31 Chevrolet Special Coupe
RUMBLE SEAT
CASH PAYMENT **$140.00** Balance Arranged

1929 Durant Six Sed
CASH PAYMENT **$125** Balance Arranged

1928 Willys Knight
CASH PAYMENT **$10** Balance Arranged

1929 Durant Co
CASH PAYMENT **$** Balance Arranged

DO IT NOW

Drive your car in and let us put it in proper Winter Driving.

For $6.95

we will do the following work on any 4 cylinder $8.95 for any 6 cylinder car.

Grind valves, remove carbon.
Carburetor cleaned and adjusted.
Spark plugs and electrical system checked.
Distributor cleaned and timing adjusted.

BIGGER and BETTER BARGAINS

Week End Specials
THURSDAY, FRIDAY AND SATURDAY
GROCERIES

Pea Soup, National Brand	3 for 25c
Sweet Mixed Pickles	10c
Salada Orange Pekoe Tea ½'s	35c
1 lb. Tin Baking Powder	19c
Magic Baking Powder, 4 oz. tin	7c
Clark's Tomato Juice	3 for 23c
Libby's Pork and Beans	3 for 20c
Good Morning Marmalade	21c
Crown Blend Black Tea, lb.	35c
Health Bran	2 for 25c
White Beans	5 lbs. for 10c
Clark's Pork and Beans, large size	2 for 25c
Prunes, large	3 lbs. for 25c
Quick Quaker Oats, china	29c
Clover Leaf Salmon, 1 lb. tin	25c
Blue Ribbon Malt	98c

McBean & Co.
GEORGETOWN ONTARIO

The prices were often rock bottom – even so nobody could afford any luxuries.

The Depression Years

MEMORIES

No one today believes you when you tell them what it was like in the 1930s. That six cents my brother and I spent on candy in 1924, not counting the copper we threw in the river, would have bought a loaf of bread in 1933, or a small can of pork and beans.

The stock market crash that triggered the Great Depression in 1929 was the beginning of the despair that gripped the country, but in Norval it was the flour mill going up in flames in 1930 that really saw the decline in the local cash flow. Then the Bank of Nova Scotia closed its doors in 1931, the Electrical Radial Railway (Toronto to Guelph) folded in 1932, and the freight sheds on the Grand Trunk yards at Norval Station were half empty. Trucks on the highway were now hauling more and more of everything.

No longer did the farmers have to haul their heavy cans of milk to Norval Station where the train boss, the Conductor, would yell at them "Shove on your swill!" He stood on the train steps, Elgin watch in hand, impatiently counting the seconds while a hundred cans of milk were loaded on his train. Trucks on the back roads ended all that. And with tractors appearing on the farms, the blacksmith's work was much lighter. When Jim McKinney's blacksmith shop closed in the late 1930s George Day looked after blacksmithing chores but that shop, too, soon closed.

When the farmers couldn't afford to buy new equipment and their produce was hardly worth harvesting, the economy overall was in bad shape. Cattle prices hit rock bottom. A neighbor sent a cow down to the Toronto stockyards with a local trucker. The cow was old and not in great shape, but the markets that day were even lower than usual, and the trucker was embarrassed to have to tell his neighbor that not only was their cow gone, but they owed him $2.00 for the transport over and above the pittance the cow had been worth.

Pigs were selling at $3.00 per hundred weight, and to get that top price the pig had to weigh 180 pounds give or take five pounds. Underweight or overweight was an excuse for the slaughter house to take a few cents off the hundred weight price. "Select" was the grade you aimed for, the Perfect Pig. But the ultimate consumer paid top prices across the board for his bacon, no matter whether the bacon was from "the little pig who went to market", or the pig who "pigged out" at the trough.

The grocery stores in the 1930s took a beating. When the storekeeper knew his customers as old friends, and also knew their financial circumstances, he would carry them over on credit, but the grocer also had bills to pay. A day of reckoning came for everyone; sometimes the store had to close.

A page from the local Georgetown Herald in 1934 revealed the sad story: three tins of soup for 25 cents, granulated sugar was five pounds for 25 cents, sausage was two pounds for 25 cents, good salada tea was 40 cents a pound and baking powder was 25 cents a tin. The Magic Baking Powder had coupons in it, as did coffee, and for 50 coupons you could send away and get a baseball — and that was a big item. The baseball bat came out of the woodpile.

For many years we had a tea merchant who came twice a year from Galt and delivered tea to the homes. His name was T.C. Dorner. He would have several hundred pounds of tea and coffee shipped from his home in Galt to Norval Station, and, having previously arranged for a horse and buggy, he proceeded to deliver the orders. It took him about three days to cover the area. Mother always welcomed him with a cup of fresh tea and a scone or what-

John Slingsby and Alex Gregg help raise the barn – an act of optimism in the 1930s when a good farm could be bought for as little as $20,000.

ever, and in return he gave her a wee bag of whole nutmegs. Finally he bought a car, a reliable Model T, but he was never at ease with it, and sat bolt upright at the wheel, doing his best to keep it from running away. With a horse he could relax and enjoy the ride. Then came the day when the 1930s got him too. We missed his visits. He was a dapper little man, always so neatly dressed; he had a clipped English accent, a goatee and was always most grateful for any kindness shown to him.

In the 1930s there were lots of bargains in land and housing. In the Norval area a good farm, 100 acres, with house and barn could have been bought for $20,000 or less. Even at that there were some farmers who had no hope of meeting their mortgage payments and they just walked off the land in quiet desperation. Some business people, too, lost absolutely everything. For those people who had financial reserves, a good farm could be picked up by paying the back taxes to the municipality. I don't remember any suicides around there because of money problems, but I recall a 1930s newsreel in the theaters that showed stockbrokers jumping out of windows in New York. Life had become impossible to face.

On the whole, though, farmers fared better than most. There

were no luxuries, you patched and mended, especially the overalls, and you stored all kinds of fruit and vegetables for winter. Cabbages were hung by the roots in the cellar, carrots went into boxes of sand, potatoes and turnips into a bin in the cold cellar and apples were kept in barrels. The mangels (a course kind of beet) and turnips for the cattle went into a pit dug in a hillside that was roofed over and covered with a deep layer of dry straw. As needed they would be put through a root pulper, which had a wicked blade and was turned by hand. We called the root pulper the "Guillotine". The cattle appreciated the fresh taste on their dry feed, and we always ate a slice of raw turnip too.

Parsnips left in the garden till spring were so good, sweet and tender, the frost having taken all the bitterness out of them. There weren't any freezers in those days, so you preserved and canned everything you could: berries, peaches, pickles and often meat.

Pig killing was a dreadful day. The pigs didn't like it and neither did we but it had to be done. Pork could be salted, cured and hung in the cellar. You cut the bacon off a side when you needed it, parboiled it for a few minutes to get the salt out, then fried the bacon slowly. Those were the days when a ham was big and round, not one of those long rectangles cut off square pigs, and spareribs had plenty of meat on them. Homemade headcheese with home-ground horseradish was special too. And if the pig had a little extra fat on his bones, we made doughnuts, dozens of them, and put them in a crock. Their life span was always shorter then we expected; they didn't keep very well!

One of the biggest concerns we had in the 1930s was to make enough money to pay the taxes. To be in arrears was to risk everything you had worked for; it was touch and go. When help for corn-cutting and threshing was needed Dad always paid cash. He said the labourer was worthy of his hire and if you couldn't pay his wages you shouldn't ask a man to do your work for nothing.

Hughie Clark looked after the threshing needs for many farmers in the community. Combines hadn't yet appeared on the average farm, and often the wages for his labour were very slow in coming. At one point in the 1930s Hughie was heard to say he "would just like to have a new suit out of his season's work!"

Maybe he did — or maybe repairs for his tractor took priority.

And when your grain was threshed and safe in the granary, oats brought 25 cents to 30 cents a bushel in 1935, and wheat, literally the gold standard of agriculture, went down to $1.00 a bushel. One dollar, for sixty pounds of grain — and you waited a year for the cash. The wheat was planted in late September and harvested the following July, that is if the Hessian fly didn't get into it because it was planted too early, if it didn't winter kill or smother under ice, if it got the right amount of rain in June to "fill" the grain and if it wasn't flattened in the field by heavy winds and rain when it was ready to harvest. Not to worry? A farmer has to be an incurable optimist or the world would have long since collectively starved to death.

We had a market garden venture during the bad years. We had planted an acre of asparagus, which has to be down for at least three years before you can start cutting it commercially, and then only lightly. We called that acre the "backacher." We sold the asparagus on Guelph market for five cents a bunch or 10 cents a pound, carrots washed and cleaned for 15 cents a six-quart basket, onions and beets for 25 cents a basket, apples the same, and on other stands you could buy 50 pounds of good potatoes for 50 cents.

Those were the years, and the war tears too, when we could not have managed without Lil Morris' help. She could pick and pack anything. We would be in the orchard for weeks at a time; the apple trees were high and old in the Upper Canada College orchard which we had rented. The apple trees were later replaced with Canadian forest trees.

A crafty vendor turned up at the market one Saturday with a truckload of what he called "Snow" apples, a well known variety everyone enjoyed. The apples were the right size and the right colour but Snow apples they weren't. They were the Ben Davis variety, hard as the hubs on your wagon and good keepers, so good that in two years you still couldn't cook them. The vendor sold out quickly and we didn't see him back on the market until the following spring when he brought in a full load of geraniums. He separated them into blocks on his market space and labeled the blocks red, white, pink, or whatever. None of them were in bloom but the price was right, 15 cents a pot. A customer asked him for two pots of the "Martha Washington" variety and he seemed puzzled but only for a second. "Certainly, ma'am, we just happen to have a couple left." So he went to the other side of the truck, picked up two pots out of the nearest block, handed them over, accepted her money with thanks, then turned to his helper and said "Now who the h— is Martha Washington?" The scam wouldn't be apparent for a month and the vendor figured any flower was worth 15 cents.

Jobs were so scarce in the 1930s that a man would gladly work for a dollar a day, plus his dinner and often his supper. In the worst years a live-in farm worker earned perhaps fifteen dollars a month, with board and laundry. When the crunch was on, about 1936, a summer helper was offered his board to tide him over the winter with the understanding he would lend a hand with the chores.

Girls could not find work for which they had been trained. Teachers and nurses particularly were thankful to find jobs in shops and mills, and others settled for domestic, maid-of-all-work situations which could be pretty grim by times. All the

The 1930s were, more than usual, a time when "making do" was the watchword – pictured here the frustrating work of mending a broken grain binder.

washing, waxing, cleaning and meal preparation for a family of four was worth $15 a month, with just four hours off every other Sunday. One girl I knew kept food on her mother's table and coal in her stove on that $15 a month and she took only $1 for herself. Such workers felt the injustice but hardly dared to complain.

Eaton's catalogue was the handiest store when you didn't have a car. Mother would phone an order in and it would be delivered two days later. Work socks for the men were five pairs for $1, and underwear was $3.00 a suit. At some point in the 30s Mother ordered three "hard wearing woolen suits" for Dad. Father declared it was woven from barbed wire and barley straw — barley awns are murder in a shirt. He threatened to burn the lot, but Mother said repeated washing in soft water would help. It was a vain hope. The underwear didn't wear out but it did disappear. That bit of the worldwide depression was just the last straw for Father.

By the mid-1930s household linen cupboards were getting pretty bare and everything needed mending. However, sugar and flour came in factory cotton bags which could be ripped open, washed in soft soap to try to take the printings out, and four of them sewn together to make a passable sheet. Mother went over the seams with embroidery cotton in a blanket stitch. The bags made pillowcases too, and the finer ones were hemmed for tea towels. It was just a question of "do what you can, where you are, with what you have." However, through it all we didn't go hungry, just had the odd case of the "wants": wanted cornflakes instead of wheat porridge every morning, wanted an orange instead of another apple, wanted a chocolate bar instead of another spoonful of honey. But as I write I realize again how very fortunate we really were. Dad used to bring in a bushel of wheat and we ground it fresh every day. It made good porridge but young people like a change, and we often wanted shredded wheat or cornflakes, which we called baled hay and shavings.

The local churches had a hard time paying their bills, too. The minister's stipend suffered from delays and the N.S.F syndrome at the bank. The following was found in a Clergy residence, about 1937, when the wallpaper was changed; it had been written on the living room wall, perhaps in a moment of depression or defeat:

> *"I hope that one day I may see*
>   *A warden who will hand to me*
> *My stipend on the day it's due*
>   *For that's thing they seldom do*
> *A stipend to sustain my needs*
>   *To carry on with words and deeds*
> *A stipend that will buy some gas*
>   *As through my parishes I pass,*
> *A stipend to give to those who ask*
>   *For help to aid them in their task*
> *A stipend oft in vision viewed*
>   *A hope deferred, sometimes renewed,*
> *The people here have wealth they say*
>   *But only God can make them pay!"*

About 1932 or 1933, my brother Warwick and I were offered a trip to the Royal Winter Fair in Toronto by a neighbor, Mr. Linham, who drove an old Ford Touring. It had buttoned side curtains to keep out some of the rain, the snow and the cold, but half the buttons were off and it was near the end of November. But we did enjoy the day: the Mounties Musical Ride, the prize cattle, the butter sculptures, and the Dale Estate Autographed roses. At least one leaf on every stem was marked with a perforating stamp, "Dale." It was because of the extensive greenhouses, Dale's had almost fifty acres under glass, and Calvert's about the same, that Brampton was known as the "Flower Town" of Canada.

But it was that cold uncomfortable ride home, in a snowstorm, I will never forget. Such bone-chilling misery, it seemed to symbolize everything that was wrong with the world in those Depression years. You just had to ride it out and trust there would be better days ahead.

Today I am glad we went through those years. We appreciate everything we have now but we never take anything for granted. Life can change in a single day.

Lament For a Farmer's wife, 1935

For forty years in wedded state they farmed the land together,
She fetched the cows and slopped the pigs in sundry kinds of weather.
He drove the team and ploughed the fields and helped out in the stable.
But never, ever, offered once to even set the table.
Her garden was a picture, though ne'er a rose was in it
Potato blooms and pumpkin flowers were just about her limit.
She mowed the grass and pulled out weeds, and oftentimes she pondered
Why so many chores were "hers" or had she sadly blundered
The wood-box was a daily stint, took hours to cut and fill
She didn't mind the outside chores but they left no time to kill
No time to read, no time to sew, no time to rock and think,
Just time to do the dishes – and no confounded sink.
She'd mentioned water in the house and then perhaps some plumbing
To ease the weekly washing and to save her feet from running —
The tubs were getting heavier, the kettles felt like lead,
He said "we'll do that next year, seems we'll never get ahead".
But then, the horses needed harness, the cows a lot more meal
Though the pigs would pay the taxes, the shortages were real.
She had three dozen chickens who might grow into hens
And lay some eggs for other folks — to help her meet both ends.
And then there was the broken fence a lively calf ran over
And got himself two stomach's full of ripening wheat and clover,
He didn't want to leave the field, in fact he wouldn't budge
Nor would he ever move again no matter were she nudged –
Oh well, there'd be a calf to sell, another year, another day
But it did upset their plans for buying extra feed and hay.
The oat field has been too wet to plant, the hay too long in soak,
And come the Fall it really seemed the farm would be plumb broke.
He took it hard when setbacks came, she did her best to cheer him

And never said she'd counted on a carpet for the kitchen
Or a cooler for the milk and cream, the butter, pies, and jell
Instead of that old bucket she pulled in and out the well.
And then one day, oh boy, oh joy, she saw him leap the bars
Across the lane, his feet just flew, his eyes lit up like stars!
He'd found a spring, a lovely thing, it looked like oil, not water
And smelled like money in the bank, no more his purse would matter –

That night he counted out his wealth – on paper – tens and fifties,
He'd buy a truck, a car or two, fix up the farm real nifty
He'd roof the barn and build a shed, paint the milk-house all in red,
All this he planned with ne'er a thought of that tired woman in his bed –
He knew that she would understand a man needs tools to work his land,
And come next spring if all went well he'd put some pipe in that old well
And if a sink was what she wanted, he'd price one where a dollar counted.
Yes, she knew his good intentions but also knew she wasn't well
The time had come for her to just sit back and rest a spell –
Or maybe after forty years the worm had made a little turn
And whispered in her ear "you're worth every cent you earn."
But the knowledge came too late, her body was too worn
Her heart had broken twice in life and she wouldn't see the morn.
When he found her cold but smiling he felt most awful strange
As if she hadn't really left and would soon be up and at the range,
I thought she'd like to drive my truck, fetch the feed, have a ride
And now she's gone and left me, shucks, I wish she hadn't died.
The road ahead looked long and bleak, he'd never meant to be unkind,
But it's hard to shake off poverty when its sits there on your mind,
But now that wealth had come his way the gold had lost its glitter
For he didn't know until she'd gone just how much he would miss her.

M. (C.) M.

After the Depression – The War Years

*W*e are the generation that was born during the Great War, grew up in the devastating Depression of the 1930s — the Dirty 30s — and faced a second World War while still in our twenties. Those years shaped our lives and because of the impact of that Depression and the War that followed it, we have never taken anything for granted in life and have an immense appreciation for everything we now have. The sorrows of the Second War seared out minds and left scars that will never disappear.

When the Armistice signaled the end of the First War in 1918 I can remember hearing the factory whistles in Georgetown and the Norval mill bell and the school bell ringing in celebration, and to hear them even better I climbed up on a fence post. I also saw my first airplane. I had just turned four.

When the Second World War broke out in 1939, for the first time in Canadian history every citizen had to be registered, and your registration card had to be carried on your person for the duration of the War. By 1941 we had to apply for ration books, with coupons for butter, meat and sugar. The sugar allowance was one half pound per person per month and bacon about the same. Gasoline was also rationed but the amount depended on your work; the government was a trifle more lenient with farmers as production of food was a high priority for the outcome of the war. Experienced farm help was difficult to come by and many farmers had to rely on students from the city. On the whole they were good boys, but most had never mentally made the connection between the milk on their city table and the cow in the farmer's barn. The work was an eye-opening revelation to them.

World War II brought another kind of hardship – rationing.

Two months before war actually broke out in 1939 the British Government issued a pamphlet "If War Should Come" which was also distributed in Canada. The threat of war was in the air and although assurances were given that it was just a possibility we were advised to procure gas masks and make sure we knew how to use them.

On September 3RD, 1939, when a state of war was declared between Britain and Germany, our world changed forever.

Within the week, Canada declared her support for Britain. Recruiting centres for Army, Navy and Air Force personnel were quickly set up and the Commonwealth Air Training Schools and Flying Fields were established all across Canada. Air Observer, Pilot, Bombing and Gunnery Training Schools were everywhere. The first graduates from Malton No. 1 Air Observer School, (later changed to Navigator School) were a class of New Zealand boys, and from the Toronto Island Airport boys from Norway learned to fly. Sadly, two of them crashed at Norval Station on a training flight. So many families, thousands of miles away as well as those closer to home, received telegrams that said: "We regret to inform you….."

Two of the village boys, Gordie Browne and Bud Carter were taken prisoner and spent many months in a Prisoner of War Camp in Europe. The war was getting closer to home. Then red-headed freckle faced Jimmie Louth, R.C.A.F. was killed when his plane was shot down, and Flt. Sgt. Tony Leach, born on our home place in 1921 and working as a rear gunner on a Halifax bomber

Roy Coupland, RCAF in barracks at Torbay, Newfoundland, 1941.

Joan (Browne) Carter, Canadian Women's Army Corps, 1944.

was reported "missing" after a raid on Hanover. Flying Officer Roy Coupland on Coastal Patrol duty off the coast of Newfoundland and Labrador told us later just how close the enemy submarines were in the Gulf of St. Lawrence. Don Murray made twelve hazardous trips over the North Atlantic with the Ferry Command, delivering Canadian-made planes to Britain. Squadron-leader Terry Evans was a valuable instructor at Trenton Air Base, and Surgeon-Lieutenant Stewart MacDonald served in the Royal Canadian Navy.

Bill Carney, Air Mechanic, R.C.A.F. was burned so badly while servicing a plane at Bagotville, Quebec, that he didn't survive and was brought home to be buried in Hillcrest Cemetery in Norval.

Ray Whaley with the Engineers was in the forefront of the liberation of Holland. Bill Pierson, Jim Clark, Fred Humphrey, John McClure, Ernie Driver and Mac Hunter were in the R.C.A.F. Captain Edith Loree (Nursing Sister), Joan Browne, Ted Louth, John Rankine, John Dunlop, Jackie Graham, Clifton Moreton, Irene Hazel, good old Red Roshier, Freddie and Wes Fendley, Winslow and Erni Beamish and Doris Adams were all in the army. Harvey Davidson, also in the army, died in England.

In August, 1946 there was a parade of Norval veterans led by the Pipe Band of the Lorne Scots, from the corner of Adamson and Guelph Streets to Norval School. Colonel Louis Keene, Commanding Officer of the Lorne Scots, presented engraved watches on behalf of the community and village of Norval to the men and women of the area who had served their country in the Armed Forces. Unfortunately, not every one received a watch as contact with some could not be established.

In every Province a Memorial plaque was erected in one of the National Parks to honour the memory of all those who did not come home. Usually the plaque is set in a chunk of granite with the words cast in bronze relief:

"They will never know the beauty of this place,
See the seasons change,
Enjoy Nature's chorus.
All we enjoy, we owe to them,
Men and women
Who lie buried in the earth of foreign lands
And in the seven seas."

The following is a letter written to Joy Laird from a sailor to say "Thank you" for a ditty bag she had packed. All through the War the mail was censored, opened and read. The point origin was never identified, so the letter starts:

Jackie Graham (left) off to the war in Europe.

*Can't say where
But it's New Years*

To Dear Joy
Whoever blessed you with your name must have known what kind of a nice little girl you would grow up to be, spreading rays of sunshine for us who go down to the sea in ships, all of which tells you of the joy and delight I experienced on opening the ditty bag packed by you. It is hardly possible for me to say how much I appreciated it.

It would take too long for me now to answer your poem round by round, perhaps I will be able to later but I will say that the ditty bag was not as black as you painted it and we were even able to eat the candy, believe me it was good.

No doubt the war will be over before you finish school, otherwise we would sure be glad to see you in the W.R.E.N.S. Personally I would be glad to see you anytime.

I am giving this to one of the boys to post as I can't do it myself very well, so I hope you will get it sometime (I stole this paper and grabbed the chance of the office machine, boy will it ever be a wonderful feeling to get back to civilization again).

*Love for now, more later
and thanks an awful lot.
Jim*

Joy didn't hear from him again. Maybe he was one of the many who did not come home.

Long after the guns are silent, the music of a war is remembered. Men and women may march to a different drummer, but they make their music their own. In the 1920s we were still hearing echoes of the Great War: "Its a long way to Tipperary," "We'll never let the old Flag Fall," and "Pack up your troubles in your old kit bag and Smile, Smile, Smile." An entertainment group called "The Dumb Belles" did a tremendous service for the men in the trenches of France.

In the Second War, the songs were a bit more personal: "Don't sit under the apple tree with anyone else but me," "Give me one dozen roses, just one dozen roses, and send them to the one I love," and "Praise the Lord and pass the ammunition." Vera Lynn sang "There'll be Blue Birds over the White Cliffs of Dover," and "We'll meet Again." And there was the strange phenomenon of a haunting melody sung by a husky-throated German girl that had the Armies on opposite sides of the battlefield singing along with her. The song was "Lili Marlene." Bing Crosby's "I'm Dreaming of a White Christmas" and "When the Lights go on again all over the World" hid a lot of homesickness.

It was in "our war" that women deserted the kitchen and took to the factories and the Armed Forces. "Rosie the Riveter" (remember that song?) worked in shipyards and aircraft assembly and ammunition plants, drove streetcars and buses, and worked all over the country on dairy farms. Camps were set up in gardening and fruit growing areas and the girls lived in tents for weeks at a time. That getting-out-of-the-kitchen movement was the beginning of a minor revolution. Family life changed when mothers didn't stay home, but in the years of that brutal war the women pulled their own weight and their help was of tremendous value to their country.

CHAPTER FIVE

A Life on the Farm

The author's beloved Home Place, built in 1828. Pictured here in 1926 with gingerbread porch and pine siding

A Life on the Farm

Charlie and the Home Place

"Lilac Hill" is located on the west half of Lot 12, Concession 6, Chinguacousy Township, County of Peel, Old Ontario.

All over this country you can read bare bones facts, like the above, about old home places, but every one of them has a story to tell. The past has a way of projecting itself into your future; your former footsteps leave an indelible mark on your memory. So it has been with me.

If Captain Curry could come back today he would find his old home sitting as comfortably on its foundations as the day he put it there in 1828, all of it built of sturdy white pine. The Captain chose the site wisely, several hundred feet back from the road, safe from future road widening. Superficial changes have been made, inside and out, but the original structure is solid. The Captain added a new part in 1867, a large pleasant kitchen.

The first residence on the farm was a log cabin, half way back to the next concession, probably built in 1818 or 1819. It was located on a knoll beside a spring creek and when working that field we found pennies of 1811 and 1817 vintage.

When Henry Pettigrew bought the farm about 1875 he added a small front porch with gingerbread trim, a back stoop and a separate shed beside the house which was used as a summer kitchen. The Pettigrews retired to Toronto in 1919.

Major J.O. Leach, a veteran of the Royal Flying Corps in the Great War, bought the farm from Henry. The Major, despite having lost one leg in an air crash in France, made many improvements, particularly in the house. He deepened the stoned well by

The windmill erected by Major Leach in 1920 – when the wind blew it saved hours of pumping water.

another hundred feet, erected a windmill and installed indoor plumbing and bathroom facilities and a kitchen sink which is still in use. The Major loved the farm but his heart was in flying, so in 1922–23 he sold the farm to Charlie Coupland, my father, and joined the Forestry Fire Patrol in Northern Ontario. He was killed when his plane went down in Thunder Bay in 1929.

When Dad took over the farm there was no proper stabling, just tie-up room for a few head of cattle on the barn floor. Both barns, built of white pine in 1840, sat on the ground. You have already heard about the outside building jobs and now Charlie was about to tackle Captain Curry's old home.

In digging out the whole cellar of the house the men discovered the original foundation for a fireplace which had been removed at some point, probably when a kitchen range became available. The outside covered entrance to the cellar was replaced by inside steps, which necessitated building a porch to house the new steps and also to protect the kitchen from the north winds.

Warwick coming up the back lane with the last load of rakings – gleaned off the field once the stooks were gathered.

Dr. Clark Noble's young children enjoy the great swing that Dad made for us.

The plaster on the living room ceiling was badly cracked, so Father knocked it all down and exposed beautiful hand-hewn virgin pine beams, twenty-four feet long and as sound as the day they were hewn. Finding those pine beams was a real bonus in the renovations. To reinforce the ceiling, Dad squared two red oak timbers, notched them and with good help they were raised and locked into place across the pine beams. The spaces between all the beams were then replastered.

Making good use of the fireplace foundation that had turned up in the cellar was a satisfying project. The new fireplace was rebuilt of fieldstone from the back of the farm and the stone came into the living room in a wheelbarrow. Mother said she had lived in sawdust and shavings all her married life but a stone hammer really tried her patience. But the improvements were always worth the upheavals. Dad took great pains to shape the keystone just right for the arch at the front of that fireplace. He also put a crane in it and made the fire dogs in the shop. The iron basket for the burning wood came from an old threshing machine.

The water system Major Leach had devised was workable but awkward. There was a huge 300 gallon tank the length of a room upstairs, lined with heavy galvanized tin and fitted with a wooden lid. There was also an overflow pipe through the outside wall but we still had to be very careful about shutting the windmill off or the tank could have overflowed upstairs. However, when good stabling was put in, the big water tank was moved to the barn.

Because it had been built inside the house there was no way to get it out except through the window, which was far too small. Dad figured if he had to make a double window in one room he might as well do them all so he put in casement windows. And while he was at it he also put a wide, low window in the "dark room" where Captain Curry's wife used to hang cured meats, safe from the flies. All the early pioneer homes had a dark room or a dark corner closet.

An interior view of the Home Place, 1938/39 – the coal stove dates back to the 1880s.

The stairs in the house had long been a problem with jackrabbit steps, steep and straight, so Father reversed them, made them wide and easy, with a landing part way up. Off that landing he cut a half door into the kitchen attic and added a window there too.

Kitchen cupboards had been non-existent for over a hundred years, (a cabinet with shelves stood on one wall) so, using butternut and pine, Dad soon had cabinets and clothes space where needed.

When we decided the outside of the house should have a coat of stucco, Andy Frank did an excellent job and it did make the house warmer. That same summer a new stone verandah was built across the front of the house. And on top of the kitchen roof Dad built a belfry and restored the farm bell to its rightful place. We had found the bell, buried in straw in one of the old barns. The bell rope came down into the kitchen and

Farm bell on the kitchen roof.

we would ring it about 11:45 a.m. to give the men time enough to come in from the fields and feed and water their horses. The horses soon got on to that bell themselves and would head for home. The neighbor's horses listened for that bell too and Mrs. Cameron phoned my mother one day to ask her not to ring it so soon; her men were coming in before she had the dinner ready.

There weren't too many furnaces in farm homes in the 1920s. We had a kitchen range with a waterfront in it to heat the hot water tank, and a Quebec heater in the large downstairs bedroom. That type of stove could become very hot, and chasing my little brother around it one day he got too close and blistered his bottom. I got a blister too but not from the stove.

The old reliable source of heat was the tall self-feeding coal stove in the living room, with doors with mica windows all around it. We lit it in late October and it didn't go out until late April or even May. We sat around that coal stove on winter evenings listening to the radio and eating apples: Spys, Greenings, or Tolman Sweets, Seek-no-Furthers and Scarlet Pippins. Every year we made a new small hole in one of the mica panels to push the apple cores through. We had to make a new one every year because Father would always find the old one and mend it. What a comfort that coal stove was. The soft, safe glow when you came in from skating still warms my memory.

The coal stove took two skuttles of coal a day, one in the morning, another at night. If the temperature went down to 20 below zero we would top it up at midnight.

Chimney fires were not uncommon in wood stoves and we had one that I haven't forgotten. It happened on a Sunday morning. Mother was away visiting my brother Bob in Nova Scotia and Aunt Sara Glendinning had come to help out in Mother's absence. Aunt Sara was getting ready for church. There didn't seem to be much to eat in the house so I fired up the range with hardwood chips and put two pies in the oven. The oven got very hot and there was an ominous roar in the stove pipe. Sure enough, the chimney was on fire. Said Aunt Sara, "So you baked on Sunday, so the chimney is on fire, so get up on the roof and put it out. I'm going to church." Which she did.

From the roof I watched her walk down that road with a never a backward glance, and I couldn't help being very proud of her. Her church principles and Victorian upbringing would never let her do unnecessary work on Sundays. We all fall short in that respect. We loved our Aunt Sara; she really was a dear little woman and was wonderfully kind to four young people in our house.

We walked a great deal in those days, up the river, or to the back fifty, and Dad would tell me that the delightful fragrance in the evening dew was wild grape bloom, or a Sweet Briar not far away. There were real bluebirds back then who nested in old fence posts and we kept track of their numbers. The killdeers would nest on open ground and Dad and the boys dodged the nests when they were working the fields. I don't think tractors care about killdeers.

There are so many reasons whey I owe my Father a very large debt; important, but often intangible reasons. When I was eleven I sat on a pile of straw on the barn floor beside him as he cradled a heifer's head on his lap. She was dying of blackleg but we didn't know till later what had happened to her. All Dad could do was stroke her cheek to let her know she wasn't alone. When I was ten he lifted me up to show me a hummingbird's nest, built on the

Dad preparing to install a stable window, early 1930s.

crotch of a flat twig, with two miniature eggs the size of beans in that beautiful moss-lined nest. Dad planted hundreds of trees. He said you didn't plant trees for your own generation, you planted them for the next. And you must not burn out a field with chemical fertilizer but use all the manure the farm produced to keep your land in good heart.

When Dad top-grafted older apple trees, he went up the ladder and I went up the tree. My job was to keep the beeswax soft enough for him to cover the grafts. We didn't have tree dressing in cans in those days. Roy and I both learned to graft too.

Dad taught me how to identify forest trees, fruit trees, apples, leaves, barks and weeds. And we shared one of Nature's little jokes. So often, when you find a Sweet Hickory in the bush there will be a Bitter Hickory within a few feet of it. The sweet and the uneatable side by side.

When we were very young Dad found a baby crow that had fallen out of the nest, brought him home and we fed him chopped meat and oatmeal. That crow was a plague to my mother; he would take the clothespins off the line of washing and hide

Roy Coupland and a friend with a "tree run" of Northern Spy apples ready for market, 1939.

Roy (Jack), age 12, cultivating with spring-tooth cultivator, 1929.

spoons under rhubarb leaves. He was really great fun. When cold weather came he wouldn't stay in the porch, he preferred the hitching post in the yard and one night an owl got him. Poor old Jim Crow.

Dad came out to Canada in 1903 with his chum Will Stringer. July that year was a scorcher. Dad's employer said "Charlie, take that woolen underwear off or you will collapse with the heat." Dad took his off but Will said, "What keeps out the cold will keep out the heat." But it did not work that way. In three weeks Will died of heat stroke, and he is buried in the fifth line cemetery (Chinguacousy).

In England Dad had been apprenticed to a rope-maker at the age of fourteen, had obtained his certificate at twenty-one but decided there had to be more to life than making a million miles of rope. However, during the past war he found his rope experience was very useful. Good rope was hard to find, and Father made tow ropes, sling ropes, leads and halter ropes, all out of binder twine. He could also splice ropes when a knot wouldn't go through a pulley.

Dad and Mother enjoyed their home and were most generous

in sharing their talents, their time and their table. Mother fed anyone who came to her door hungry and we had a good many of those during the Depression.

In the 1930s my parents were asked by a friend on the 10TH line, Mr. Walter Brian, if my Mother would cook a turkey he would provide, and would she also ask several of the local farm help, boys from England and Ireland, to share the dinner. No problem. Mother stuffed that 25 pound bird and served it with all the trimmings. At the end of the meal Walter said he had enjoyed that turkey more than anybody, for he had fed him good grain all summer and fall. In fact he had fed all of Miss Broome's turkeys with his good grain and apples because those turkeys just wouldn't stay home. So Walter "adopted" one, put him in a granary with extra food and water until the day of reckoning came. "Fair was fair" said Walter, "Miss Broome owed me that one." My dear mother wasn't so sure.

Those were good days when we were all at home. Life revolved around the farm, the church and the community. You needed your neighbors and your neighbors needed you; interdependence

The boys who enjoyed Thanksgiving supper, 1934 – and Walter Brain's "adopted" turkey.

and sharing the work load welded the community together.

Looking through Dad's line-a-day diary, I found the following:

"Oct. 21, 1914, Baby girl born this morning. Dug turnips in the afternoon."

I had just arrived. On one line!

The Stable Door

*M*emories, memories, where do they start when you are a child growing up on the farm? Was it the first time you held a half pail of milk and fed a calf, was it at three when you leaned against a cow and milked a whole cupful of milk for yourself, was it when you were considered old enough at four to be trusted with the important job of opening and shutting the lane gate for the teams hauling hay, or was it at five when your mother sent you out to the field with a cold drink for the men stooking wheat?

So many memories. You didn't realize you were being eased into the work force on the farm. Farm children accepted responsibilities very early, chores were a way of life. Somebody had to keep the woodbox filled and take out the ashes, somebody had to wash the milk pails and the cream separator, somebody had to make sure the water-trough was always full and turn on the windmill. If there wasn't enough breeze to turn that huge fan you pumped the water yourself, but the water-trough had to be filled somehow. So you just did it.

That is not to say that as you got older the hum-drum chores were not a drag, but the nurturing of your livestock was paramount. Anyway, it was a pleasure to hear the horses greet you with a soft whinny when you opened the stable door, and to see the calves come to front of their pens looking for a friendly pat on their head.

We had four horses, two teams: Danny Boy and Jenny, Daisy

Joy Laird and Geoff Noble at the stable door – Geoff was a fun-loving and invaluable helper on the farm during many a long summer.

Horses Queen, Danny Boy and Jenny hard at work bringing in a heavy crop of Victory oats.

and Queen, and later, a team of black Percherons, Bonnie and Baker. Bonnie and Clyde would have been more apt. We got them as three-year olds; they had been raised together as colts and never separated. They didn't like other horses or strangers in the barn, but they loved to work and could out-pull and outlast any team in the neighborhood. They were easily spooked and would take off with, or without, just provocation.

At stook threshing one morning I took out a large bottle of Tansy ale to the men at the stack. It must have been shaken up a bit on the way for when I took the cap off the first bottle the ale soared in an arc over the backs of the big team; they took off like rockets and ended up in the woodpile behind the implement shed. Warwick, forking off sheaves, was caught off guard and couldn't reach the lines. So much for that tea break. We let the other bottle settle a while.

To make that brew you steeped yarrow in boiling water, added sugar and a bit of yeast and let it work for a week or two before bottling it. It was a refreshing drink on a hot day. My grandmother's generation made lots of things, medicinal and otherwise, from what grew in a fenceback.

Dad would never let an aged horse leave the farm alive. He

said "The horses have given us their best years and no one will get a chance to abuse them in their old age." When Baker went down at twenty-three years of age and had to go, Bonnie spent the next three months with her head over the partition of Baker's stall. Then she, too, left our stable. A sad time for everyone.

Our cattle were all purebred Jerseys. Dad had purchased two yearling heifers through the Canadian Jersey Cattle Club about 1921, and with several additions and natural increase we had a very nice small herd by 1930. They were all tuberculosis free, tattooed with our herd letters "A.E.C." and all registered under the "LILAC HILL" name. Almost without exception they were a golden cream colour. City folks would ask "How on earth do you tell them apart?" "That's easy," we said, "we know them like you know your own family." The cattle all had names, on paper, but when you had to ask them not to stand on your foot they only answered to gentle persuasion and a swat on their rump. We didn't have any cattle privileged to wear a silver locket on their forehead. That honour was reserved for animals that were born on the Island of Jersey itself.

Until the mid-1930s Thompson's Maple Leaf Dairy in Georgetown bought their sweet cream from the farm; the surplus went to Morris Saxe's creamery in Georgetown. Mother also made butter.

When we started shipping milk to Canada Dairies in Toronto, we had regular visits from a milk inspector, and for some years that inspector was Major Forsyth. He came in, swinging a cane, wearing a trench coat, giving a creditable impression of an English army officer, which he probably had been. On one such visit he left a note on the stable door, "Charlie, you have more windows in this stable than I have in my house. Good. Now get those cobwebs down." We used a pine limb for that job. It worked fine.

Farm signs represent a real achievement and ours meant a great deal to Dad and Mother.

When you have a herd to maintain you are constantly on the alert for signs of distress among them. Clover is excellent feed but too much of it on a damp morning can cause bloat (acute indigestion) and if you don't act fast a cow can die in agony. It was hard to drench them and harder still to use a trocar, an instrument to puncture them in that little triangle in front of their left hip bone, and release the gas that was killing them. Just finding the right spot to use the trocar was very difficult when the swelling was so immense that even their hip bone would disappear.

Lil Morris (later Garbutt) our all-round help for years – Lil would pick and pack anything that grew, she even scuffled corn!

We had an apparent case of bloat one evening. A heifer was showing great discomfort and we realized she was actually choking. A small green apple had lodged in her throat; it wouldn't move with massage and even when Dad propped her mouth open, my small hand could not get far enough down her throat. The heifer was getting quite upset, and our veterinarian, Dr. Bill Bovaird, was eight miles away. At that point an English neighbor, Mr. Linham, appeared at the barn door, heard the difficulty and said "Charlie, get a stout plank and a mallet, I'll hold her tail to one side, two of you hold the plank hard against her buttocks, then you, Charlie, 'it that plank one 'ell of a swot." We all did what we had to do and the apple flew out across the stable floor. It was a close call for that nice little heifer. Mr. Linham had been raised in an apple-growing section of England. Perhaps a similar problem had arisen there as he knew exactly what had to be done.

We used to feed the calves cod liver oil. Some of them liked it and others would dodge it, just like kids. The oil gave them a little boost, especially in the winter.

When we brought the cattle in from the pasture for milking, they all knew their own stall. There were very few milking machines on the farms in those days and until about 1939 or 1940 all the milking on our farm was done by hand. The full can, with

80 pounds of milk and 20 pounds for the can, was carried out to the milk tank which was filled with ice and water, and an extra block of ice was added to keep the milk well chilled. The large blocks of ice, cut from the Norval mill pond and later from our own pond, were stored in the ice-house in deep sawdust for summer use.

There was one very special cow who would appear at the barnyard gate about half-past four so she could go with me to get "those other cows." "Happy" she was by name and by nature and in memory too. Father said I had spoiled her with too much attention; after all she was just a cow, one of the herd, but "Happy" and I differed with Father on that assumption. The tie-up line appears now on the page in keen recollection as it was in that stable: Peggy, with her crumpled horn; Delphine, the leading lady as they walked up the lane; little Lightfoot, who at least once a month forgot her manners and put her FOOT in the pail and me in the gutter; Sybil, the aristocrat; Barbara, so pretty with a white star on her darker face; Olive, the old matriarch and mother of many; Rebecca, gentle Rebecca; Debora, who would steal Rebecca's meal; pleasant little Fanny, and many other sweet faces of the past.

For some years, like Henry Pettigrew and Major Leach before

Some of the herd in fresh pasture, 1940.

us, we lost one or two head of the yearlings every year, generally when the pastures were short towards the end of summer and the cattle inadvertently picked up soil with the grasses. When you keep livestock you realize they can become dead-stock very quickly. What was killing the cattle was "Blackleg" and the germ seems to live in the soil. Once the germ was ingested into their system that animal was doomed and would die within forty-eight hours. First she would go lame, and then if you ran your hand over her thigh the skin crackled; that was the beginning of the end. In the 1920s we would bury the cow on the farm with a great quantity of lime in what turned out to be a vain effort to halt the contamination. When a vaccine became available we injected a Blackleg "oid" (a very small tablet or pellet) under the skin before they went out to pasture in the spring. That injection meant one worry less on your mind.

Roy (Jack) at the shop door – some harrows sit to the left of the door waiting to be pointed.

We still had to contend with bloat, lightning, green apples and water hemlock. We pulled the hemlock out of the creek and cut down the wild apples. Milk fever could be controlled, but if mastitis was a problem we didn't have the drugs in the early days to cut down the losses.

During the war years one of our student helpers could not remember which cows had to be milked, which cows were "dry" (between lactations) and which cows got the most meal. So I dipped the milker's tails in green paint. Father was not too pleased but the deed was done. Three days later the lad asked "Do we milk the green tails or the black tails?" More green paint, this time on their backs where they could not lick it off.

When Dad bought the farm in 1922–23, there was no proper stabling for winter shelter, just a dugout under one end of the barn. So Dad had a "bee" and Alfred Laird, Murray's father, lined

This sad little heifer reflects the prevailing mood on the day the herd was auctioned, 1959.

AUCTION SALE
of
43 Reg. Accred. Vaccin., officially
blood tested
JERSEYS

the property of

C. W. COUPLAND
Lilac Hill Farm, Lot 12, 6th Line, Chinguacousy, quarter mile N.E. of Norval (No. 7 Highway) on

TUESDAY, MAY 19th at 2 o'clock
DST, the following
20 cows, some fresh, several bred for fall; 14 heifers bred for fall; 9 younger heifers.
This is an outstanding home-bred herd, every animal raised on the farm. Good sires of popular blood lines have always been used, and unit sires for the past 3 years. Fully accredited since 1935. Every animal in herd positively selling, as Mr. Coupland is going out of the milk business.
Milking machine, Surge 2 unit milker, with piping for 27 cows.
Terms Cash.

FRANK PETCH,
Auctioneer
Telephone TR. 7-2864
George Currie, Clerk.

the men up in teams, and when Alfred called "yo-o-o-heave" the men lifted the timbers into place. One day's teamwork saw the frame and the rafters all up and long before winter there was stabling ready for all the stock. This first stable was later converted into an implement shed. With additions to the herd every year, the next big job was raising the main barn and the pea barn and pulling them together to make an L-shaped stable. Lloyd Davies of Brampton did an excellent job of raising and moving the barns. Dad and the boys built the thick stone walls with stone from the back of the farm. It was a long, hard summer's work. But when it was finished we could tie up thirty head, had box stalls for young cattle, a well-reinforced bull pen, a number of calf pens, four horse stalls and a "maternity ward," an extra box stall. There was now ample room upstairs for all the hay and straw we would need and good granaries for wheat, oats and mixed grain.

The "pea" barn was the barn where Henry Pettigrew stored his large crop of peas and in the winter when they were very dry, he would fork them onto the barn floor and thresh the peas out with a flail, two pieces of hardwood, thicker than broomsticks, looped loosely together with a leather thong, end to end. We kept the name, having heard it for so many years.

Then, after almost forty years, there would be no more golden Jerseys on "Lilac Hill." The sale was in 1959 and beef cattle came into the barns. You often shed tears when a cow died, but when the herd was sold and I knew they were gone forever, I wept for them all.

The Farm Pigs

We liked our pigs on the farm. They always had their own quarters away from the cattle and seemed to enjoy what always turned out to be a short life. Given half a chance, pigs will keep themselves clean. They love to eat, they like a dry bed, and enjoy a good wallow; other than that their wants are few. Would that people could be so easily satisfied.

We kept one brood sow, sometimes two, and there would be two litters of little pigs a year. On average they would be ready for market in five and a half to six months. Mr. Wade Toole, B.S.A., in his publication on Breeding, Growing, and Finishing the Bacon Hog writes, "When a Select reaches his majority, which is usually in about six months, he is long and smooth with a nicely arched back and a straight, trim, and neat underline." You could say the same thing about that new car in your garage.

A litter could contain any number up to ten or even twelve piglets, but then the nursing facilities were taxed to the limit, and you ended up bottle feeding one or two. Little pigs are cute and they are smart; only when they are older do they get a bit pig-headed.

Our old Sukey was specially fond of apples. Mother gave her a treat one day and nearly polished her off prematurely with two buckets of crabapples, but she did survive.

The pig yard was not too far from the wooden silo, and a couple of weeks after corn cutting there would be a run-off from the fermenting corn. The pigs got into the bubbly and acted just like people, in similar circumstances.

Dad liked Yorkshire pigs; they were solid and dependable. The Landrace breed was beginning to appear in the 1930s, they were longer-bodied and produced more bacon per inch than other types. The Canadian market is not keen on sow-belly pork so you wouldn't find too many fat old pigs loafing around on the average farm.

For some reason, difficult to understand, public opinion denigrates a pig while he is alive, but when he is dead he is SOMEBODY! He is the pride of an English breakfast, the centre of a Canadian dinner, or the epitome of Southern hospitality as Virginia ham.

A pig's life is necessarily a short one, but when you had fed the little pigs for months and taken much pleasure out of watching them grow and develop definite personalities, it was hard to see them loaded into a truck and hear them squealing their resentment as they were driven off the farm. They most surely had my sympathy on that trip.

Oats as far as the eye can see, 1936 on the home acres.

The Seasons of the Year

"HARVEST HOME"
"We plough the fields and scatter the good seed on the land,
Where it is fed and watered by God's almighty hand.
He sends the snow in winter, the warmth to swell the grain,
The breezes and the sunshine, and soft refreshing rain."

So we did — but spring seeding was never as simple as it sounds. The horses got extra oats starting in February to build them up to be ready for the heavy work ahead. The fields had been ploughed the previous fall, loads and loads of manure spread on them in the winter, and as soon as the land was ready in April or very early May, the manure was cultivated into the soil with a spring-tooth cultivator, raked over with harrows to smooth down the lumps, sometimes twice over, to provide a good seed bed for the grain. If you owned a roller this was the time to use it. Finally, if the weather held fine the seed drill was loaded with cleaned grain which had been put through a fanning mill well in advance of seeding. The fanning mill had a different screen for every type of grain, and shook out weed seeds, or anything else that might plug up the outlets on the seed drill. The drill could be set to release a given amount of seed per acre, whether you were sowing oats, wheat, barley, buckwheat or mixed grain for future chop. Now if the dust was blowing and the spring rains were slow in coming, the last implement over the sown field would be a packer, a very heavy low roller, which pushed the seed just a little further into the ground. Because the soil was by now so finely worked, the moisture in the ground would rise to the surface; the old theory of capillarity at work. Having gone through all this in three or four fields, you waited to see if the promise of a harvest would appear — and it did. There was an old superstition years ago that if you missed sowing a drill width there would be a death in the family that year, but I don't suppose anyone ever tried to prove it.

If the weather turned hot during this heavy work you had to watch for sore shoulders on the horses and put seat pads under their collars; you depended on those horses all year round.

The last crop to be sown was usually the corn, which was more susceptible to a late frost than any of the grains.

While all the seeding was going on, the hay was growing and the pastures had been greening. If you put the cows out too early the pasture didn't get a chance to thicken up. You could usually start haying by the 10TH to the 20TH of June. Hay was cut with a mower with a 5- or 6-foot blade, then raked into windrows and left to dry for a day or so. Then the windrows were piled into cocks, miniature stacks, and left again to dry. When it was ready for the hay mow you piled the haycocks onto the hayrack and

The packer leaves its tracks on a seeded field, 1941/42.

then into the barn. So far, every move was done by hand forking, but once in the barn, you used a hayfork suspended from a track in the ridge of the barn to lift the hay into the mow. As the hay was levelled in the mow, again by hand, you sprinkled it generously with salt to help in the curing and act as a fire retardant; if the hay overheated, spontaneous combustion could burn the barn. It almost happened to the Cameron's barn one year. The weather had been "catchy" and the haying was a bit rushed. It smelled great, as only new hay can smell, but as the week wore on the smell became sinister. There was something very wrong in the haymow. No plume of smoke could be seen; there was no sound in the barn, no fire anywhere. But later in the winter, digging that hay out, the Camerons found a blackened cave deep in the mow. The fire had started, but the depth of the hay had choked off the oxygen.

Over the years we have seen too many barns go down in flames. Several burned at threshings when a piece of metal accidentally went through the machine, causing a spark that would ignite the dust. The men in the mow would have five seconds or less to get out of there. Lightening was always a hazard. Bill Reid on the third line west lost not only his barn but his herd as well, on a stormy night. And there was always spontaneous combustion to be reckoned with. If hay was damp when it was brought into the barn it would overheat and cause real trouble.

From our hill-top home we could see for miles, and over the past years have witnessed at least fifteen barn fires, three of them next-door neighbours: Archie McMeekin's, Bert VanVliet's and Murray Laird's. Other barns that have burned belonged to Joe Hunter, Don Bull, Bill Hyatt, Jim Clark, Joe Bianchi, Art Ruddell, Gordie Laidlaw (both the original and the replacement), Carl Laidlaw and Ed Greensword (his had been empty for years).

The list and the losses are staggering. When the older barns were built they probably cost $3000 to $5000. To replace a modern barn today, complete with good stabling, a farmer is facing a minimum of $300,000. For many reasons, fires are what farmers have nightmares about.

Haying could take two to three weeks, then you might have a

little break before the wheat you had planted the previous fall was ready to cut, around July 20TH to August 1ST. We had an old "Frost and Wood" binder. Binders are heavy implements to pull and always needed three horses. The sheaf carrier held eight to 10 sheaves and they were released at short intervals where the stooks would be made up. The stooks, gatherings of eight to 10 sheaves, could stand for several weeks if they were well made. Again it was all hand forking on and off the wagon until we had "slings", four sets to a wagonload, which could be lifted into the mow on the same overhead track as was used for the hayfork. When it was threshing time, the sheaves all had to be forked out again. In the

Jeff Needham on the buckrake, 1949.

1930s, Dad and the boys built a buckrake on a 1928 8-cylinder Parkard which was built like a tank, and at a stook-threshing in the field the buckrake was a real labour-saver. The fork could scoop up a dozen stooks and whip them back to the threshing machine in minutes. In the late 1930s combines were appearing, and a farmer who had one would do "custom" combining; your grain was cut, threshed, and trucked to the mill all in one day. The weather was specially important for combines to operate efficiently — the drier the better.

By Canadian National Exhibition time, towards the end of August, the oats and barley would be ripe for harvesting, and this time the grain would be stored for feed. Wheat was a cash crop, as were portions of the other grains.

A threshing bee in the barn needed at least a dozen men, three or four in the mow, one on the feeder platform, one in the straw stack, two shoveling in the granary, one or more with the machine, and perhaps several who would just turn up in case they were needed.

Corn cutting in late September or early October was handled very differently. A special cornbinder could cut one row at a time, and drop the sheaves one at a time. They were very difficult to stook, or 'shuck', so usually you tried to arrange the field cutting the day before the cutting box was available. For the corn, you needed five or six teams, five drivers, six men to load, two to unload, two to tramp the corn in the silo and often two at the machine. Corn cutters, working in the open, were hungry enough to enjoy a good meal and my mother set a good table at any time. A 20-pound rump roast went in the oven for noon; there was huge bowls of creamed, mashed potatoes, carrots, tomatoes, pickles, tea biscuits and pies all up and down the length of the table. Matt Laidlaw used to say "Mother, two cents worth of dog meat would have lasted longer than that roast."

The corn-cutting supper table was cold meat or a roasting pan full of sausage, a mountain of fried potatoes, pickles, biscuits, muffins, more pies, and tarts. One young lad, new to the country, spied the long line of pies on the table and decided meat and potatoes could wait.

Jack Garbutt with his cutting box that handled our corn for years – Jack was killed on his next job when the sleeve of his new smock caught in the machine.

A funny little episode is remembered about a corn-cutting. One good soul, who was *very* frugal, baked custard pies on a Friday for the promised corn-cutting bee. But it rained, and it rained on Saturday, too. So she put the custard pies in the cellar, which was damp. Sunday was fine but you never did outside work on Sundays. Monday was fine and up came the pies from the cellar. Their hired man, back in the kitchen for a moment, saw what was happening with the pies, went back to the field and warned the men "Don't eat them pies, or you'll be sorry, the Missus is in the kitchen shaving them." Custard in bad storage conditions will grow green whiskers, and besides, could kill a fellow.

Jack Garbutt's cutting box handled our corn for years, and when he came in one year he had a very ragged smock. Dad paid him cash when he finished his job and Jack said "Charlie, you are the first man who has paid me this fall. Now I can get a new smock. I'm afraid the ragged sleeves on this one will get caught in the cutting box." The very next farm he went to, the new smock got caught. The new material wouldn't give, and Jack died at the foot of the pipe with a broken neck. A farm can be a very dangerous place.

Somewhere between the oat harvest and the corn, you could cut a second crop of hay, or let the seed on the clover ripen and cut it much later and thresh it. Peel County was famous for its clover seed in the 1920s but one year for some reason, the seed wouldn't "set". The only explanation ever given was that a trace element in the soil was missing from overproduction in previous years.

The turnip crop suffered a similar fate because of a lack of Boron in the soil, also a trace element. The turnips developed a brown heart and didn't keep very well over the winter. We harvested the mangels and turnips very late in the fall, often in mid-November, pulling them up, cutting the tops off, and storing them in a pit or in a cement room built under the barn dump (the ramp leading to the drive floor over the stable.)

In planning the crop rotation for the year, Dad planted the corn and roots, (turnips and mangels) in a field that had a lot of weeds. And because corn was a "hoe crop" the rows would be twice hoed by hand and several times scuffled by horse. All of which helped to clean the field. When the corn was nicely up we went down the field, three or four abreast, weeding as we went. Infinity was closer than the ends of those rows; there is no word for that kind of tiredness. Once the fields were cleaned we turned our attention to the burdocks in the fence-backs, which we removed with a spud; a short, sharp blade mounted on the end of a long handle.

The cattle were stabled for the winter in late October or early November depending on the weather, and from then, til early summer the stables had to be cleaned out every morning, hay and straw brought down from the mows so the cattle could be fed and bedded down, and the silo opened for the daily ration of fermented corn. For a long time the gutters were cleaned out by shovel and wheelbarrow. Then in 1929–1930 Dad got some track that had been discarded after a fire, straightened it out and hung it from one end of the stables to the other behind the cattle, and another section of track in front of the mangers for carrying feed. Then he made two carriers; the work was so much easier after that. We still had to lift the manure but not wheel it.

Our dear neighbor Hilda, a newcomer to Canada from London, England said to a local farmer "Well, now that the cattle are all in the barn for the winter you won't have anything to do, you'll be able to travel!!" Dear Hilda came to love and understand our Canadian ways, and was much loved in return.

Anytime after the middle of January the ice on the Norval mill ponds was thick enough to harvest. Cutting ice was a cold, wet job and lifting the big blocks onto a sleigh was heavy work. All farmers had an ice house and an ice refrigerator. To preserve the ice you packed it in sawdust which you had hauled from a lumber

T.L. McMeekin and Warwick hauling ice from our pond – fences were cut to shorten the distance across the fields to the icehouse.

Mother supplies Warwick with a cold drink while mowing – our first ice house is in the background.

company or saw mill. The trick in getting a block of ice out of the sawdust was to remember where you had left off, for the sawdust was knee-deep.

And somehow, in between everything that went on in the fields and the barn, you had to make time to mend the fences, make them "hogtight and horsehigh", prune and spray the fruit trees, and cut and stack enough wood for the coming year.

Then in 1935, when we figured we were about due for a break, Father decided we should have a farm pond. A lovely clean creek ran diagonally across the whole farm, touching every field but one; an ideal situation for pastures. Digging the pond out was done by team and scraper, the cement wall crossed from one gully hill to the other, and there was a 10-foot head of water at the spillway. The pond lasted for years until muskrats got under the wall. It was a good swimming hole and a great place to skate.

But the pond served us well. When ice was no longer being cut on the mill pond in Norval our neighbors depended on our small pond, until coolers appeared in the milkhouses.

There never seemed to be any time on the farm to sit back and take it easy, and for many farm people back in the 1920s and 30s, holidays were what other people had; chores and crops took precedence. But you accepted the situation, partly because you didn't know there was another side to life.

But when I look back, we had the best side, and I wouldn't trade those years on the farm for all the tea in China.

Dad on his 80th birthday, 1962 – Charlie Coupland, 1882–1970.

CHAPTER SIX
The Community Beyond Norval Village

Norval Grand Trunk R.R. Station – David Russell (left) waits for a train.

The Community Beyond Norval Village

Norval Station and Post Office

The old Grand Trunk Station of 1854 at Norval was located a mile and a half north of the village and around 1900 was a very busy commercial centre. The station master's home adjoined the waiting room and the ticket and telegraph office. The large freight sheds and holding corrals for livestock were in constant use with the stock heading for the Toronto stockyards.

Herb Jackson was the first station agent I remember; he was said to be the best telegrapher on the line. His sister Florrie could also handle the Morse code on occasion to give Herb a break. She was a nurse and her last twenty working years were spent as Head Nurse in the Infirmary in the Royal York Hotel in Toronto, starting the day the hotel opened.

Prairie Maguire, Dr. Sam Webster's niece, used to tell of an old couple who had decided to send a crate of eggs and a firkin of butter to their cousin in Toronto. They got it packed up, hitched the horse, drove to the station, put everything in the baggage car, and were just leaving when the baggage man noticed there wasn't an address on the parcels. He quickly asked "Where's this going?" but the dear little lady just smiled at him and said "It's all right Mister, they know it's coming." Off they drove, thinking what a nice surprise their cousin was going to find at the station. They had sent her a card but didn't tell her what to look for on the train.

We can almost understand that pair ourselves these days. At eighty-three your brain isn't always in gear!

The Post Office at Norval Station served a wide area. The first Postmaster was John Bird and the Post Office was in his home, several hundred yards north of the station. When he sold the house around 1913, the new owner Arthur Morris, became the Postmaster. The Office was closed in the late 1930s. Much later the home was torn down and a new home built on the lot by Art and Carol Sweezie.

Mrs. Watkins, John's mother, operated a coal business from the coal sheds at Norval Station. Good nut coal was under $5.00 a ton, and you hauled your own. There was no delivery available. When Mrs. Watkins got older, the Newns brothers, Norman, Bill, and Harold, were a good help.

The Watkins' home, directly across from the long gone freight sheds, is still there, beautifully preserved. It is now owned by David and Julia Bagshaw, who really appreciate their heritage home, built in 1885.

The boys of summer in the 1880s – Harry and Joe Hunter; Frank, Ted and Bert Robinson, amongst others.

Two brothers who married two sisters – Tom (top left) and John Bird with wives Sara (top right) and Effie (McLean) Bird. John Bird was the first postmaster at Norval Station, he retired in 1913.

John Watkins of Norval Station

John Watkins was born in 1902 at Norval Station, Ontario and attended the lower 5TH line public school and Brampton High School. He was an extremely clever boy with a real flair for languages. He taught Scandinavian Studies at the University of Manitoba and in 1946 he joined the Department of External Affairs. Being fluent in Russian he was sent to Moscow as chargé d'affaires from 1948–1951, then to Norway as our Canadian representative there. He returned to Moscow as Canadian Ambassador for several years and later went to Denmark in the same capacity.

John Watkins had a brilliant career. Unfortunately his death at age 62 came about as the result of unproven allegations concerning his years in the diplomatic corps. John is buried at Norval.

Whaleys Corners and the Old Town Line – Upper and Lower

In 1819, William Coulson Whaley, an Irish immigrant with a family of five children settled on 100 acres; Lot 1, Concession 11, Esquesing township, the northwest corner of the intersection of the base line and the townline (now Steeles Avenue and Winston Churchill Boulevard.) In April 1840 he received the Crown Deed from Queen Victoria which is still in family hands.

In 1844 William opened a tavern and also started a blacksmith shop. By a pre-nuptial agreement in 1860 William deeded the land to his second wife, Mary Ann McCracken, and when William died at the age of 93 in 1869, Mary Ann signed a "Surrender of Ease" handing the property back to William's son, John Whaley, in 1889. Five generations of Whaleys have lived on this farm, four of them actually farming.

Today, Raymond and Kenneth Whaley and their families still reside on parcels of the original farm, most of which had been sold in 1971 by their widowed mother, Lena.

Ray and his son Gary operate heavy equipment, specializing in constructing fine golf courses. At present they have twenty golf courses to their credit with enticing names such as Deer Creek in Ajax, Lakeridge Links in Uxbridge, Emerald Hills and Spring Lake, both in Stoufville, The Glencaster Club in Mount Hope, Indian Wells and The Oakville Executive, which are both located in Milton. Ken, who taught high school in Brampton, is now retired.

All seven children of Gordon and Lena Whaley still look to Whaley's Corners as home. It has always been just a great community.

Yarns from Whaley's Corners

The Post Hole Stripper

The original log home at Whaley's Corners – an early stationary hay baler stands in the yard.

The sheer pin in the new auger was just a small one. Gordon Whaley got tired of buying new ones, so he cut a six-inch piece out of an old rake tooth and used that for a pin. It did the trick but stuck out past the shaft. Digging post holes one day, Gordon, for some reason, bent over the auger. The bib of his overalls caught on the rake tooth, the auger kept turning and peeled off his overalls and shirt like you would peel a banana. Fortunately Gordon's work clothes were quite worn and tore easily or he would have been turned inside out in ten seconds flat. Lorne, who had been on the tractor, ran to the barn for a bran sack, and with a section of mower blade from the tool kit on the tractor he cut two holes in the sack so his dad could step into it. Gordon, shaken by what had happened, yelled to Ken (age 9) who had been watching the proceedings, to run to the house and ask Mother for another pair of overalls. "Dad wants another pair of overalls," said Ken. Mother replied, "What's the matter with that man, he put on a pair of clean overalls already this morning. Tell him he can't have any." Back to the tractor went Ken and told his dad, "You can't have any more overalls, Mother said so." Again Ken was sent to the house with the same urgent message. This time Mother came out herself. Sizing up the situation, she decided another pair of overalls at that moment would be a very good idea.

A Hay Ride at Whaleys' Corners

*I*t was haying time, the hay mow was filling up and Mr. Whaley wanted to change the draw rope pulley in the peak of the barn to the other hay mow. So he made himself a sling with a board in it and hooked it to the pulley that lifts the bundles up to the hay car. He needed to be pulled up to the hay car by the draw rope, which was attached to the bumper of an old 1937 Chevrolet car that didn't have any brakes, so Mr. Whaley had already put a block of wood behind the car wheels. 12 year old Lorne Whaley was in the car and had been told to take it easy. When he got the word to let the car roll down the dump, Lorne turned on the ignition, which he wasn't supposed to do, and the old Chev got away on him. Father shot up to the hay car in the peak of the barn and flew across the hay mow on the car track. The draw rope broke and Father sailed out the end of the barn, hit his head on the stop-block and hung forty feet in the air, bleeding all over the place. Then the sand bag ballast attached to the hay car pulled it back to the block above the centre of the drive floor. It tripped itself, and Father, tangled up in his makeshift sling, came down pretty fast and landed on the bare barn floor, really bleeding by then, and only half conscious. The boys knew they had to do something quickly. There was a bucket of water handy and a pail of salt beside it. The salt was used in curing the hay. Kenneth and Keith, being kids, had been busy putting the salt in the water bucket, for no good reason, but it looked as if their dad needed some cold water to wake him up, so they threw the salted bucket over him. The salt in the wound on his head revived him with a jolt. Mrs. Whaley patched him up temporarily and the Doctor in Milton finished the job. It could have been a terrible tragedy, but fifty years after the fact the boys see only the funny side of the trip their father took when he rode the rails in the roof.

The Lower Town Line – Norval South

I have purposely covered this section of the old Town Line in some detail, mainly to show how interwoven the community has become over the years, the old with the new, maintaining many of the old traditions and family values of the past one hundred and fifty years.

The Town Line, part of the first plank road from York to Guelph, was the only access road to the northern part of Esquesing and Chinguacousy townships. You will still find some of the pioneer names on today's mailboxes: Whaley, May, McLaughlin, Smellie and Hunter. The Hyatts and the Harrops have only recently left. The Jack Humphrey farm, was sold in 1951–52 to Bill Laidlaw after Jack's only son Fred died when his tractor caught fire. The farm ownership dated back to 1837.

On the north corner of the intersection of the Town Line and #5 Sideroad, now Embleton Road, Charlie Burton's house still stands, on or about the former site of the "Dew-Drop Inn." His daughter Eleanor operated a fruit stand on that corner for years.

The McLaughlins came in 1828 from Plum Bridge Ireland, and one of the McLaughlin's later homes, built in 1888, is now the Croatian Centre.

When the Thompsons arrived on the Town Line they lived for several years in their original log cabin, which had been covered with siding and painted white, but inside there was still a ladder to

Cattle going home for milking along the Town Line South – sometimes cattle were pastured on the road side. The fence was made of good pine boards.

the sleeping loft which was the usual arrangement in the early days. The new brick home, now owned by the Branders, was built in the 1920s.

The Grahams came to the Town Line after the First World War, and their home is now occupied by Dr. Rogers.

Above #5 Sideroad the heavy clay soil changes to sandy loam which is ideal for market gardens. In the 1920s Joe Bianchi arrived and bought ten acres from L.J.C Bull. He did well on it by dint of hard work, and raised a family of seven. Now Joe's son, Walter, owns L.J.C's farm and grows apples and berries. The community is grateful for Walter's strong support of local hockey teams.

Keith Webb came up from Prince Edward Island in the early 1940s, and he and Ethel have a greenhouse and florist business. We have never forgotten the commercial pansy patch along the front of their property. What a treat to see. Keith is a brother of Marion Laird and his roots go back to the Lucy Maud Montgomery connection.

Edward Smellie, grandson of Jennie (Bird) Fiddler and also grandson of Mr. Ed Smellie, built a new home on family-owned

The original Robinson home on the Town Line South was formerly a church.

land. Marie Murray, daughter of Mr. Ed Smellie also lives on her home acres. Don Murray, a cousin of Marie's born on the 10TH Line, built his own home on the Town Line.

Bert Snow's strawberry patch is now under Ken Arnold's greenhouse, and new homes have been built on Bert's potato ground. But across the road, Bert Snow's nice natural stone fence still stands.

Geoffrey Noble, son of Warwick Noble, and great-grandson of Robert Noble of the flour mill, built his home overlooking the Credit Valley. Mitch Hunter lives on Hunter land. The original Robinson home, the converted Disciples Church, was bought in the 1940s by the George Smith family, and Don Smith still lives on a part of his home property.

The Thomas Forster farm, owned for many years by Joe Hunter, is now the home of the Matsumerid family.

Hillcrest Cemetery has been considerably enlarged over the years, and Mrs. Collin's hospitable old home is long gone. The Wiley family were the last to live in it on the hill. Only the pump, still in the well and still in use, marks the site of the original Presbyterian Church. A frame building, it was an integral part of the heritage of the village. The old Collins home was brought down the cemetery hill and put on a foundation in the lee of the hill across from St. Paul's Parish Hall. Extensive renovations produced the present fine home.

Other lines and sideroads reveal the same pattern of a fairly stable resident population over the years. The village on the other hand, with the exception of a very few families, has become a dormitory for people who love their country homes, but whose work, of necessity, is often miles away in cities and towns.

Just crossing the concession lines for a moment, there was a special industry on the 9TH line, a brewery, started by the Brain brothers who arrived in the 1830s. They had some brewing experience and made ale for the family but had so many requests for a glass that they developed a real business. The first brew they made was nearly 80-proof, but they finally got it down to 29-proof; still a fairly potent draft.

The fine old Brain homestead, beautifully restored by Fred and Clara Robertson, was bought by an artist who, out of deference to its beginnings, name his home "Brain Manor." A thoughtful gesture.

The Upper Town Line – Norval North (on Winston Churchill Blvd.)

The upper Town Line above the village, including the blind line, was very sparsely settled compared to the lower half. The blind line, which now has no outlet to the highway, just had the two houses on it which my father had built eighty years ago for Granddad Glendinning and themselves, with a carload of lumber costing $600. The blind line now has a dozen beautiful homes on it, but the senior residents are the Millers, in my grandfather's home. Gordon Miller was a prospector who had travelled miles of the Canadian north on foot for over fifty years.

In the 1930s the only home occupied in a full mile was our own. Now there are seventeen homes. If the roads were blocked with snow you just ploughed them out yourself.

When our home place was sold in 1972–73, the house lot was separated from the land. The farm was bought by Andrew Timar, a Landscape Architect, and the home by Joe and Janet Pokluda, who in 1976 sold to a Scottish couple, John and Clova Anderson and their family, Henry, George and Tyrenney.

Mr. Timar built a beautiful home in the main barn, upstairs, utilizing the virgin pine beams and timbers, hand hewn in 1840. He built a stone fireplace with stone from the back of the farm. The stabling was renovated for office space.

Around 1990 Andrew sold the land, and as of 1996 a new family are in his home, the Kuzniars, also landscapers.

Mrs. Robinson was a mother of seven – and midwife to many women.

CHAPTER SEVEN
Old Timers Remembered

In the late 1920s and early 1930s a wonderful cast of characters donned costumes to stage an annual Old-Time Concert – Lucy Maud Montgomery (standing front left) was the cast's coach.

Old Timers Remembered

Dr. Webster, The Country Doctor

Dr. Samuel Webster arrived in Norval in 1865, fresh out of Toronto University Medical School. He had been born in Ireland and came to this country in a sailing vessel with his mother. As a very young man he worked as a journalist and later as a pharmacist where he developed an interest in medicine and went on to university. Not too long after he had hung up his shingle in Norval he started to build his own home which he called "Hope Cottage." Over the years he added a wide verandah, a carriage house and stable for his horses, his buggies and the cutter, and a windmill to pump water for both the stable and the indoor plumbing installed in the house. That windmill was the only one ever seen

Dr. and Mrs. Webster (right) entertain in their parlour, 1895.

in the village before, or since. The doctor's house was elaborately furnished and was really a beautiful home.

In 1892 Dr. Webster married Isabelle (Belle) Gollop, daughter of Mr. and Mrs. Eli Gollop, and they travelled to the Chicago World's Fair on their honeymoon. Long years later we were given the white linen dress with lace inserts that the doctor had purchased for Belle on that trip. It is worn in the village these days on formal occasions, along with an 1890s hat trimmed with violets, roses and ostrich feathers (plumes).

A country doctor in those days faced road conditions that were horrendous but it was said that Dr. Webster never refused a call, even though his practice extended from Brimstone in the north, to Bronte in the south, from Brittania on the east to Nassagawaya on the west, and all points in between. When he had a critically ill patient he stayed overnight and his horse was well cared for. When folks couldn't pay he just crossed out the debt in his daily journal, especially if children were involved. A confinement was $5.00 and most medicines and powders fifty cents.

Dr. Webster was honoured by Queen Victoria for sagely delivering triplets, and was given three gold sovereigns which he wore on his watch chain. When the doctor died in 1927 Belle Webster gave the sovereigns to the mother who had most surely earned them. The amazing and thrilling part about the birth of those triplets was that just two years previously the parents, Mr. and Mrs. Sharpe, had lost three children to Black Diphtheria.

During a typhoid epidemic in the 1880s Dr. Webster was credited with saving his patients when others died. And because at times like that he was never off the road, no one ever criticized him for keeping a flask in the buggy. He would sleep on the way home from a sick call, safe in the knowledge that his horse would find his own stable.

Dr. Samuel Webster, wearing gold guineas presented to him by Queen Victoria after he delivered triplets – after his death in 1927 his wife, Belle gave them to the triplet's deserving mother.

The Webster Home ~ a portrait of prosperity

The Webster house "Hope Cottage" pictured in 1868, soon after it was built in 1865.

This picture (circa 1890) shows the addition of front bay windows, at the rear is the new windmill and carriage house.

By 1899 the house enjoyed the shade of a mature chestnut, and had acquired additional gingerbread ornamentation – pictured are (left to right): Mr. and Mrs. Eli Gollop Sr.; Mrs. Webster; Mrs. Black; Dr. Webster; Prairie Maguire, the Websters' adopted neice; and Alfred McAndrew, who looked after Hope Cottage.

This 1927 picture shows Doris and Connie Greenwood standing in front of a new porch to the side of the house – the chestnut and original fence have been replaced by a trellis arch.

Dr. Webster's Day Books are pages of history, repeated many times. All the ills of mankind are there, and sometimes a note to say "the baby died."

When the doctor's patients were able they came to the surgery in his home, where he mixed his potions and lotions and medicinal brews. The doctor's niece, Prairie Maguire, told us a story of one old patient who was in a lot of pain with rheumatism, and the doctor suggested he take a hot bath every night. The old fellow was a bit distressed at the advice but all he said was "It ain't the 24TH of May yet." However he was back in two weeks, obviously more crippled than ever. The doctor asked, "Are you not so well, John?" Said John, "I'm fair crippled in my back, the washtub don't fit me and I told you it weren't the 24TH of May yet and its too early and too cold for the water trough." In all fairness to the stock on that farm the old gentlemen's bathtub was a discarded trough; the cattle fared better with a newer one.

The doctor and his wife had married late in life and there were no children. In 1893 they adopted the doctor's niece from the West who had lost her mother. At the Christmas concert in the Orange Hall that year the doctor introduced the child as his little "Prairie Belle." The child had been christened "Arma Mary Isabelle Maguire" but to avoid confusion in his household he called her his Prairie Belle and very shortly she was just "Prairie" to everyone. She was a total joy to the doctor who appreciated her sense of fun and her talent for painting. While Mrs. Webster was very good to her she would have preferred that Prairie had shown more interest in sewing and house cleaning.

Prairie did not marry; she felt duty-bound to care for the aunt who had given her a home, but duty is a cold substitute for a home of your own. Dear Prairie, her gift of friendship, her love and her laughter, is a legacy many of us were privileged to share, and to cherish.

Doctor and Mrs. Webster also raised Mrs. Webster's niece, her brother Eli's daughter, little Marjorie, who had lost her mother as well.

Doctor Webster retired from his practice after forty-five years, and in 1910 was made Sheriff of Halton County. In 1927 at the

Mrs. Webster in their Model T Ford, decorated for the celebration at the end of World War I – the Kaiser of Germany hangs in effigy from the back of the car, he was burned later that day.

age of 82, the old doctor died. Mrs. Webster died in 1954 at the age of 96.

Mrs. Webster loved her home and the good things her position in life had given her. She was justifiably proud of her own abilities; she made all the doctor's fine shirts, was an excellent cook and loved to entertain. To go into that old home with the deep lace curtains and velvet drapes, fine china pieces in the cabinets, Prairie's paintings of roses and pansies on the walls, cranberry lamps and gleaming silver on the sideboard and always a lace tablecloth, you wouldn't have been surprised to see Queen Victoria coming down that long rose-carpeted staircase. When hydro came to the village in 1917, Tiffany lamps and crystal chandeliers soon appeared in the doctor's house. It truly was a home you could never forget.

Some of the older people in the area still remember the doctor and his wife Belle, who was of pioneer stock herself. Mrs. Webster's mother, Mrs. Robertson, used to walk from Norval to York (Toronto) with butter and maple sugar that she traded for needles, thread and material to sew. Mrs. Webster was always fashionably dressed. The doctor was a dapper little man who always wore spats on his shoes. He was well dressed too, and always had a kindly greeting for young and old. He played a leading part in the community and delighted in local concerts and entertainment.

Today, more than 130 years after he came to Norval, he is still remembered for the care and concern he displayed for the people among whom he worked. It is a rare tribute indeed.

THE MCPHERSONS OF NORVAL

Jack and Minnie McPherson – "General" Jackson's daughter.

The McPherson's fine old home next to the Presbyterian Church was built by Henry Gooderham in the early 1850s. Henry was associated with the famous Gooderham and Worts Distillery. The McPhersons came from Inverness, Scotland and they called their new home "Inverholme."

All the McPherson men worked at Noble's Flour Mill, some of them as coopers (barrel makers). Andrew was also a beekeeper and some of his hives had thatched roofs, which was something we had never seen before. Kate McPherson was a nurse who had served in the Far East during World War I and by times she would tell us of the horrors of those days: the flies, the mud, and no antibiotics to look after the wounded. Florence was a teacher in Toronto. Mary died at twenty-one. Charlotte played the organ in the Presbyterian Church for many years, and Margaret Ann stayed home. None of the girls married, and only three of the boys, Alex, Dave and Jack. There were no children and in one generation all ten were gone.

Robert had a good tenor voice, but said he sang better when his throat was "oiled"! Jack married "Min" Jackson, "General" Jackson's daughter. The "General's" father was a military man and his son had been nicknamed the "General" when he was very

The McPherson house, built by Henry Gooderham circa 1854 – the McPherson family christened it 'Inverholme.'

young. He had a little shoe repair shop on Draper Street and the home is still there. The shop at the back was very small. Col. Noble told us that if the General got a pair of size ten shoes in to repair he had to take them outside to work on them. The Colonel often told us how the General had helped him with material for a debate when he was at school, and the Colonel was ninety-two himself when he told us that story. Min McPherson was wonderfully kind to children and young people. She always took time to listen when you needed a friend.

"Inverholme" is still in good shape and is always occupied, but chances are that box of chocolates on the small window sill beside the front door is long gone. All the McPhersons loved to have children come and visit them.

Kate McPherson's notebook of one hundred years ago suggests the following as a refreshing drink: "Dried young raspberry leaves in a tight sealer with orange peel."

Or you might want to make some liniment "for man or beast." "Mix well Oil of Originum, six ounces, and Tincture of Myrrh, one ounce. Shake and apply freely."

The eldest daughter's calling card – only she was addressed as 'Miss', the other, younger daughters were simply named.

And here is a "sure cure for gallstones"... "take Black's liver pills and three times a day drink a wineglass of pure olive oil."

"For gravel in kidneys or bladder, make a tea of Honey Bees, one ounce to a pint of water. Drink wineglass three times a day before meals."

"And this poultice," Kate said, "works every time." "Take equal parts of bran and linseed meal, mix good and thick with equal parts of vinegar and water, boiling hot. Spread over cheesecloth and over that three layers of old flannel. Will keep hot for hours, so good and works every time."

I am uncertain of the effects of that brew made with the Honey Bees. Did they know something back then that modern science has overlooked? There is a lot of venom in one ounce of Honey Bees.

L.M. MONTGOMERY

*I*n 1926, when the Reverend Ewan and Mrs. Macdonald arrived in Norval to live in the manse of the Presbyterian Church, people seemed both pleased and excited that a famous Canadian writer had come to live among us. The Entrance Class (Grade 8) was more interested in their younger son, Stewart; he was cute, he was witty and he was twelve, and we all enjoyed the new addition to our class. Stewart made lasting friendships in the village, and in her published Journals his mother wrote at different times of Sparky Bignell, Hank Rankine, Clary Hunter, Mac Watson and other youngsters.

Mrs. Macdonald took her church duties very seriously, and is well remembered by the Senior Bible Class for her weekly lessons. Craig Reid still tells you that he wouldn't miss a class when Mrs. Macdonald was there.

She was extremely kind to a group of Girl Guides in the summer of 1927. The Guides, several hundred of them, had a camporee on the Credit Valley flats on land owned by Upper Canada College, and Marion Noble had asked Lucy Maud to speak at the closing campfire. Marion called for her at the manse with a horse and buggy. Lucy Maud Montgomery stepped into that buggy dressed as she had been for royalty, and her talk held the Girl Guides spellbound. Her talk was on a shipwreck and how the Prince Edward Islanders rescued the crew and passengers. The ship was the Marcopolo.

The Macdonalds were always welcome in the homes of their congregations. Mrs. Graydon Chester tells of the time Graydon was confined to bed with a severe injury. A binder had fallen on him. Mrs. Macdonald traded mystery stories with him. She enjoyed a good mystery herself. On one occasion Graydon asked her advice about selling a team of Belgian horses of which he was very proud. A neighbor wanted to buy them, but Graydon couldn't make up his mind. So he asked Lucy Maud what she would do if those horses were hers. She said, "Sell them, Graydon. You know, one of the team might come to some harm, and then you wouldn't have either the team or the money." So Graydon sold them to Nels Robinson.

Margaret Gollop, niece of Lucy Maud's friend Geordie Gollop, had come out to Norval to visit her Aunt Belle, (Mrs. Dr. Webster) and Prairie Maguire. Margaret had been given a new copy of "Anne of Green Gables," and in telling Prairie how she loved it Prairie said, "Let's go up the street and ask Mrs. Macdonald to autograph it for you." Which they did, and Margaret remembers that visit in detail. Lucy Maud Montgomery was an extremely kind and gracious hostess; not only did she sign the

Lucy Maud Montgomery came to live in Norval in 1926, as the wife of Reverend Ewan MacDonald – here she is pictured walking on the Town Line North.

book for the child but she drew a little cat under her signature, then set the table with fresh scones and jam and a pot of tea. Margaret treasures her book to this day.

Stewart Macdonald and Sparky Bignell gave their parents and the whole village a very anxious time one winter's evening. The two of them wanted to see how far down the Credit River they could skate, and found themselves on the pond at Huttonville, which was always considered deep and dangerous. Darkness came early and the boys realized they couldn't make the trip back on skates. They knew they had to walk the six or seven miles home. In the meantime the alarm had gone out and the search was on. No trace of them could be found by the river. When they finally turned up on foot, none the worse for the long walk, they were ready for supper and for bed. Mrs. Macdonald was one worried mother that night. Stewart was the joy of her life. She had an older son, Chester, but he was already away at a boarding school, St. Andrew's in Aurora.

During her time in Norval, Lucy Maud Montgomery wrote four or five books: *Pat of Silverbush*, *Emily's Quest*, *A Tangled Web*, *Mistress Pat* and *Magic for Marigold*. Her working room was upstairs at the manse, where she could look out on the pines on Russell's hill; those trees were such a joy to her. At school we used to wonder why Stewart had to knock on the writing room door if he wanted to talk to his mother, but I guess it was the only way she could write in peace and quiet.

The Rev. Macdonald was never a well man at the best of times and there was a real scare on one occasion when he had the 'flu'. As the story was told, Dr. Paul of Georgetown had been to see him, prescribed a medication, and the drugstore had delivered it. Mr. Macdonald was resting in bed and Lucy Maud walked down the street to the post office at Barnhill's, and on her return was shocked to find her husband much worse. She described the circumstances over the phone to Dr. Paul, who got in touch with the druggist and found there had been a ghastly mistake. The only antidote for that wrong prescription was hard to come by. However, Dr. Paul happened to have just one vial on his dispensary shelf, so in great haste he came to Norval, found his patient unconscious, and sat with him for hours to see if the antidote was going to work. It was touch and go but Mr. Macdonald did eventually recover.

Mrs. Macdonald was most appreciative of her surroundings. She enjoyed her garden, loved to go for a walk, and took a great deal of pleasure with the Old-time group and the great concerts they put on in the Parish Hall.

In one of her diaries she wrote: "Norval is so beautiful now that it takes my breath — those pine hills full of shadow — those river reaches — those bluffs of maple and smooth-trunked beech with drifts of wild white blossom everywhere. I love Norval as I have never loved any place save Cavendish. It is as if I had known it all my life — as if I had dreamed young dreams under those pines and walked with my first love down that long perfumed hill."

The Credit River flats where Lucy Maud Montgomery held a group of girl guides spellbound with a shipwreck story – she wrote in her diary, "I love Norval as I have never loved any place save Cavendish."

Lucy Maud Montgomery was a fine, hospitable and gracious lady whose books have given pleasure to millions all over the world. When the Macdonalds retired from their church work, they moved to Toronto. By this time the two boys were in university, Chester as a law student and Stewart in medicine. Later Stewart joined the Navy and served as a Surgeon-Lieutenant for several years during the War. On his return he worked in St. Michael's Hospital in Toronto as Head of Obstetrics and Gynecology. He died in 1982. His mother died in 1942, and his father a few months later. To both Stewart and his famous mother, Norval was a very special place, a village that left an indelible imprint on their lives. Both parents were buried in the Hillside Cemetery at Cavendish, Prince Edward Island, their home province.

J.W.L FORSTER – JOHN WYCLIFFE LOEWS FORSTER
(SON OF THOMAS FORSTER)

From log cabin to Windsor Castle just about sums up John Forster's distinguished career. The Forster home, previous to the big brick house across from the Hillcrest cemetery, was a log cabin on the 10TH line, and in his memoirs John tells of a barn raising that almost bogged down. Mr. Thomas Forster was a strong temperance man and the neighbors had been told there would be plenty of good food but no whiskey. The neighbors gathered for the "bee" but just leaned on the fence and watched as Mr. Forster and one helper struggled with the logs. Finally Squire Menzies said to the watching group, "Let's give the boys a hand," and they all pitched in, and by supper time the barn was framed and raftered. John wrote: "The meals served that day by my mother

J.W.L. Forster home, built in 1854 across from the Hillcrest Cemetery, replaced a log house on 10th line.

(Mrs. Forster) were splendid, and at the end of the day it was Squire Menzies himself who commended my parents on the success of the 'raising', no whiskey, and no accidents. My Father served as the local preacher, Sunday School superintendent and also as Justice of the Peace."

John got his early schooling in Norval Public School where he could not resist sketching the pupils and the teacher, to the detriment of class discipline. John had been "spoken to" about this several times by Mr. Buchanan, the teacher who, when exasperated, would send a long curled up strap like a bombshell into the group. As chief culprit John would get a second strapping in front of the class. After one such episode, John was told to come and sit beside the teacher, and when the class was dismissed and he was alone with Mr. Buchanan he feared the worst. Mr. Buchanan had an uncertain temper, but what he said was, "Jown, my boy, now Jown, you know I must have order, but I want you to tell your mother, Jown, that you have to go to Rome, I say, Jown, you are to go to Rome." A later teacher, the Rev'd James Fraser, also took a great interest in John's future.

When John was fifteen he and his brother walked twelve miles to Milton to try the County Examination for teachers and they both secured their Second Class teaching certificates. Grammar School in Brampton was the next step, but the eight mile walk twice a day was too difficult for John on a daily basis. So in 1869 when he was nearly nineteen he was apprenticed to a portrait painter, a Mr. J.W. Bridgman in Toronto.

From there on, John Forster's work is history on canvas, a portrait of the times in which he lived, sketches of time itself.

John always showed a great sensitivity towards the people he painted, and enjoyed the glimpses into their lives and the historical anecdotes they shared with him. In one book *Under the Studio Light* five hundred people and portraits are listed. This book was his own biography. His second book, *Sight and Insight* lists many more of the rich and famous. His earliest book was *Master of the French School*.

John Forster's portraits are hanging in the reception room in Queen's Park, where you will find General Wolfe and General

Brock among others, painted from early likenesses.

John Forster speaks of painting Mrs. Adelaide Hooless, sister-in-law of George Lyons, who was the father of the late Clarence Lyons. That portrait hangs in the MacDonald Institute in Guelph, now associated with the University of Guelph. Mrs. Hoodless helped to establish the Institute for the training of young women in household and health education.

John was greatly taken with Sir Wilfred Laurier. "Laurier was always the statesman, with a quick, keen mind and the quality of old world chivalry." he said.

John Forster found Sir John A. MacDonald a very entertaining subject to paint. There was always a story. Sir John's patriotic vision had much to do with the framing of the Charter of the Dominion of Canada, the British North America Act, and that band of steel, the Canadian Pacific Railway, that ties the country together. The "Chief" was held in high esteem; it was said that wherever a MacDonald sits, THERE is the head of the table.

John painted Dr. Egerton Ryerson, Bishop Strachan, John Graves Simcoe, Chancellor Nelles, Sir William Mulock, the Massey family, the Eatons, Dr. Willett Miller, Provincial Geologist and President of the Mining Institute of Canada, Sir John Gibson, Lieutenant-Governeor of Upper Canada, many society figures of New York and Washington and many families in the Norval area. John Forster's portraits of Captain James Curry and his wife hung in our living room at home for years and were given to the Tax Office in the new Bramalea City Centre as a tribute to Captain Curry, who was the first Tax Assessor in Chinguacousy Township. There is also a very fine pioneer portrait hanging in a Norval area home.

John was asked if he had found different reactions to his work in different parts of the country. He said he felt the Americans were more responsive, which reminded him of the dying Scottish woman who asked her husband "Andrew, have I bin a guid wife to ye's, ye've never tellt me a word." Said Andrew in reply, "dinna think of anything to complain aboot, Jean."

In 1865, as a teenager, John would watch the Norval Company of the Halton Militia in their Drillshed across from the Norval dam. Young John made many sketches of the Corporal who was in charge of the drill. "His face and figure was so peculiar," said John, "that my pencil was immediately active." The sketches went all over the township. Forty men from the village and community had enlisted to march against the Fenians at Niagara.

Thirty years later he found himself painting Colonel George Dennison who led his cavalry in a wild dash against the Fenians on the Niagara frontier. That attack was a contributing factor in the Fenian invasion fiasco.

On a portrait tour of the west, John met a Mr. James Evans who was familiar with Norval, and was intrigued to learn that Mr. Evans was the inventor of the phonetic syllabic system based on the Cree language, by which all Indians could communicate. Mr. Evans used the lead lining from the Hudson's Bay Company tea chests to cut the letters for the printing, made his own type frame and used a hand-copying press.

John Forster, the little boy who walked our roads, went to our school, attended our churches and achieved tremendous success with his portraits, was held in high regard in Europe and North America. He was honored by universities and colleges but would find no recognition of his life's work in the village where he grew up, nothing to show that he was ever here. It is about time that Norval and the community did something about that. We have been very remiss in acknowledging John Forster's incredible talent.

Nyakawaya was an Indian orphan that John Forster loved to paint – she won many honours as an elocutionist.

John Forster himself was quite aware of the historical value of his work, and hoped that a Canadian Portrait Gallery would someday be established. To that end he left a large collection of his paintings and a sum of money in the care of the Royal Ontario Museum. That was sixty years ago. We wonder where his legacy to Canada, in trust, is now resting?

John Forster died in 1937 and was buried in Brampton. The funeral was attended by many heads of state and representatives of art galleries around the world. Even the Prime Minister of Canada was there, but no one from Norval. Shame on us.

THE EARLYS

In 1820, a young Irish couple, William and Nancy Early set sail from County Tyrone in Ireland, for the wilds of Canada. On arrival at York, (Toronto) they decided to live fairly close to the town, and so until 1823, they farmed on Yonge Street in the district known as "Hoggs Hollow." At that time the Government was giving out plots of one hundred acres to new settlers, so William got one in Esquesing township. He was said to be the first farmer to have cleared fifty acres, but there is no record of how long that took him.

William and Nancy had a family of ten children, three of whom were called Mary; several died as youngsters. William died with lockjaw at age 35, leaving a family of six sons and one daughter.

William's brother Thomas and his wife Rebecca came to Canada in 1840 with four daughters and three sons. Eleanor (Early) Holmes and her husband John, farmed near Ashgrove and had ten sons and two daughters. Another sister Rachel (Early) Moore, kept a hotel at Centreville, between Norval and Huttonville. That hotel was probably the "Dew-Drop Inn" on the corner of #5 sideroad and the town line. John Early married Ann

Part of a report of a concert organised by Dr. Webster — proceeds went to seating the Hall with chairs.

Smith and had a family of six daughters and one son.

Many of the above are buried in the Norval cemetery.

One branch of the family lived in the Owen Sound District, and once a year the Norval Earlys visited them, going by horse and buggy. If they didn't stay too long they could make the round trip in a week.

James Early, brother of Thomas, worked in Western Canada with Donald Mann, later Sir Donald Mann, on the building of the Canadian Pacific Railway across the Prairies.

The Lyons

Clarence Andrew Currie Lyons, formerly of north-west Chinguacousy, has written a great outline of his "Life and Times". Clarence's great-grandfather James came from County Tyrone, Ireland in 1835 and brought with him four sons and four daughters. Clarence's grandfather George was one of those sons, and he settled on Lot 26, 4TH line west, Chinguacousy. George met his wife, Ann Hamilton, when he was hauling wheat to Streetsville Flour Mill. His wife's sister, Adelaide Hamilton, later Adelaide Hoodless, became famous in the Women's Institute movement for her successful efforts in demanding the pasteurization of milk.

That was a landmark decision in health practice in this country. Mrs. Hoodless is credited with the founding of the Women's Institute and her old home is visited by many Institute members every year.

Clarence's brother Harold and his wife Mable (Laidlaw) Lyons, were wonderful neighbours in this community. They purchased the former Louis Laird farm at the top of Laird's hill and later bought the George Pettigrew farm across the road, built a new home on it and retired there. Their children were Edith, (Mrs. Douglas Reid) and Clark, who married Ruth (Mason) Lyons.

Clarence tells of the family's first car, a 1915 Model T Ford, a five passenger, four cylinder vehicle which cost $495.00. Clarence said "Dad drove it home and then Harold and I wanted to drive it to a Garden Party at Peter Dick's farm. Dad said 'No, it would frighten any horses on the road'. Dad drove it down the lane to turn it around, but caught his finger in the gas lever. He shoved it down and away the car went, straight into the gate post. We could hear Dad shouting 'Whoa! Whoa!' but the new 'horse' didn't listen."

License plates were $10.00 a set. No license was required for the driver; anybody who could see over the steering wheel was allowed to drive.

The Lairds

*P*eter Laird, 1807–1893, came up from Vermont to St. Catharines with his mother in 1831. In 1833 he moved on to Norval. He married Catherine Miller of Limehouse and they established a home on the west half of lot 11, Chinguacousy Township, County of Peel, which is on the townline close to Norval. His parents were from Perthshire, Scotland.

Peter and his wife had six sons and four daughters. When Peter died he deeded the farm to his youngest son, Alfred Miller Laird, (1837–1934) whose wife was Elizabeth McMaster of Orangeville. Alfred and his wife had two sons and two daughters, and when Alfred died he deeded the farm to his youngest son, Murray. Murray married Marion Webb of Prince Edward Island, a cousin of L.M. Montgomery. Murray's mother lived with them on their home place until she died.

Murray and Marion had four children: Patricia, Elaine, Ian and Peter. Elaine and her husband Bob Crawford live across the road from the homestead on a section of the original farm where they operate a very fine country bakery and restaurant. Peter lives on a portion of the home farm; the remainder of the land has been sold. The farm was in the Laird name for one hundred and forty years.

Like all the other pioneer acreages, the land was cleared working with oxen and stumping screw, but how the oxen were hitched to it we don't know. We found a stumping screw on our own home place. It was about seven feet long, three inches wide, completely threaded and extremely heavy. Does anyone out there know how to use a stumping screw?

The Pettigrews

There were five Pettigrew brothers: George (Geordie) who farmed the east half of Lot 11, Concession 6, Chinguacousy; Henry, who farmed the west half of Lot 12, Concession 6, Chinguacousy; Sam, who had a sawmill on the Credit River; John, who owned a little shop in Parkdale, Toronto; and Isaac, who lived with Geordie. Isaac had a problem and rather than have him live in an institution Geordie's sister Barbara and his daughter looked after him.

Geordie Pettigrew's favorite walk – down Laird's hill, past the Maxted home on the left, to the Post Office and general store.

My brother Roy and I were invited often to that old home. Barbara would save the Star Weekly comics for us, pages and pages of them, characters like Maggie and Jiggs, Andy Gump, Tillie the Toiler, Orphan Annie and a dozen more.

That was a most welcoming and hospitable home. I can see that kitchen yet, the patchwork quilt on Geordie's couch, Noble's mill calendars here and there on the wall, maybe five years of them, the washstand at the door, a long sideboard against the wall the kitchen range at the other end of the room. This stove was set up across a corner so there would be room for Isaac's chair in a warm spot, so that he would be out of the kitchen traffic. Geordie always kept his hat on in the house. He said it was easier to find that way. Maybe he was right.

What a fascinating kitchen that was to two kids! Isaac, with his long hair and long gray beard and watchful, piercing blue eyes looked like Jesus in our Bible stories. We had never seen a live beard before. Then there were the cats, never less than ten; that was a special attraction for us kids. We had to share *one* cat at home. The awful truth of cat control hadn't touched us at that point. The Pettigrew's cats were allowed on the kitchen dish cupboard, the sideboard, and of course the window sill. No one ever scolded them. When the oven door was down, Geordie's daughter Eileen would spread a paper on it and one old cat was given the best seat in the house.

The family always insisted we stay for "just a little bite of supper," which by times turned out to be blue damson plums with cream. The cream was inclined to curdle on the sharp acid of the fruit, but we ate the dish somehow. The big oatmeal cookies were a help. My mother would have been very upset had we refused.

Geordie was a law unto himself, one of those people who are etched in your memory forever. Geordie loved his church, his family and his land, and he loved to sing. "Onward Christian Soldiers" was one of his favorite hymns and he would belt it out ahead of, or behind, the organ. It didn't matter to Geordie, but it drove the organist up the chancel wall. And he loved the walk down that long hill (Laird's hill). He said that by listening to the wind in the pines on the Pinecrest hill he could foretell the weather. Down in the valley he crossed the Credit River on Knight's iron bridge, then took the road around the back of the flour mill and past the cooper shop. From there he went up to the Post Office and general store, Barnhill's, where he enjoyed a little chat.

Geordie told us once that his mother said he had to gather pine knots on his way home from school if he had to do homework at night, so that the fire would burn brightly enough in the fireplace for him to see his lessons.

It was the new #7 highway that messed up Geordie's life. He had been warned that he would have to give way to the cars, even though there weren't too many of them on the roads in the 1920s. Geordie said "I pay taxes on both sides of the road and I can walk in the middle if I choose." Which he did, and got away with it for quite awhile. One bad day a car came over the crest of the hill and broke his leg. Geordie spent months in a Toronto hospital and never got home again. Not only was his leg broken, but his heart was broken too.

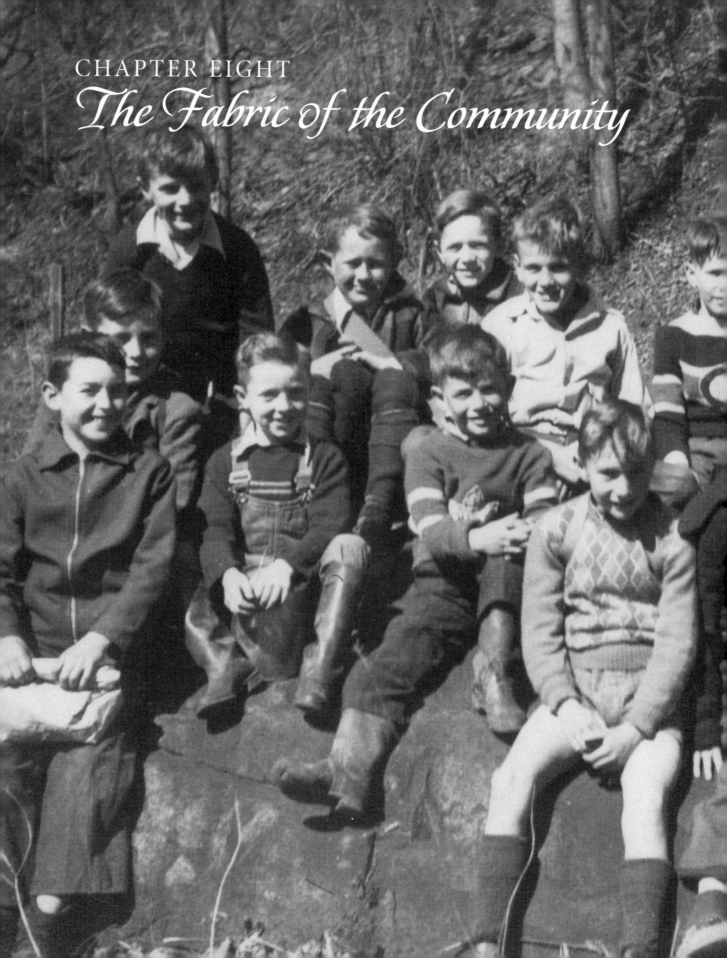

CHAPTER EIGHT
The Fabric of the Community

The author as Akela leads a cub pack on a hike in 1948 – super kids, every one of them.

The Fabric Of The Community

JIMMIE ECCLES: WORLD CHAMPION PLOUGHMAN – FURROWS IN THE FIELDS

Ploughing could be considered a rural art form. A well-ploughed field is like a masterpiece carved in the soil, a mark of excellence and a source of pride to the ploughman and the onlooker alike.

Charles Sweet, writing in the *Farmers' Digest* fifty years ago said "The soil is our heritage and we are the custodians. The soil is our most precious possession and our greatest responsibility. May God grant us the intelligence to respect the soil and the will to preserve it every way we can so that its fertility may be undiminished."

Ploughing is also a science, and without getting too technical we will try and plough one ridge — on paper. You start with a strike-out. Line up the plough with a fence post at the far end of the field, keep that post in sight between the horses' heads until you reach the headland at that post. The headland is the turning space for your team and will be the last part of the field to be ploughed. Thirty or forty feet away from the first strike-out make another in the opposite direction. Bring your team around to the inside of your first strike-out and lay the second furrow just-so against the first. You need to know how to use the coulter, or the rolling coulter, the mouldboard, the skimmer and the shares to the best advantage. Or just forget about all that stuff and settle for a rainbow plough and let it wander.

Ploughing matches have become big business and attract thousands of farm and city people every year. It is an opportunity for the farm equipment dealers to show off the newest wrinkle in modern machinery, and for farm suppliers to sell feeds and fertilizers.

County ploughing matches are held to see who will be privileged to plough in the "big one," the Provincial match, and the winner there will go to the Worlds. In 1953 when Jimmie Eccles won everything here he went to Ireland, which was the site of the World match. Jimmie represented Canada. Ploughing against eighteen countries, Jimmie came home with the "Golden Plough," symbol of the best in the world. Jimmie said he had had good coaches in preparing for that match with advice from Hughie Leslie, Spencer Wilson and George Dixon. But we all know that when he climbed on that tractor in Ireland to face that competition, it was just Jimmie and the plough, alone together.

The "smiling Canadian" had done it again!

Jimmie Eccles had a heart as big as a turnip. When he gave up raising beef, he kept two head back. When they were slaughtered he shared that good beef with his neighbours, a bushel or more to each, just excellent steak and roasts. The world could use a few more like that boy. Jimmie Eccles died in 1989.

Jimmie Eccles from Norval beat ploughmen from over eighteen countries to win the Golden Plough, symbol of the best in the world – Ireland, 1953.

Norval Kids: 50 Years Ago

*I*n 1950–51, four Norval hockey teams under the coaching of Mr. Eddie McLean, took all the honours in the local Hockey League. The community and the village showed their appreciation for this achievement by presenting them all with Norval sweaters at a banquet in the Parish Hall.

The teams were designated as Novice, Peewees, Midget and Bantams.

The smiling hockey teams on the stage of St. Paul's Parish Hall include the Coach, centre back, Mr. Eddie McLean, and the following players in random order: Bill, Ken and Jimmie Richardson, Ron and Doug Fishburn, Charlie and Peter Carney, George and Bob Grasby, George and Donnie Smith, Bill and Bob Donaldson, Julian and Laurie Reed, Jamie and Dave Cunningham, Ken Miller, Bill Patterson, Ronnie McLean, Carl Sedore, Howard Chester, Jack Lucas, Ken Robinson, J.D. Cameron, James and Sho Teramoto, Ross Cunningham.

1st Norval Boy Scout, Girl Guides, Brownies and Wolf Cubs, 1948

In the spring of 1948, a Group Committee founded the Scouts, Guides, Brownies and Cubs. The original Committee members were Keith Webb, Don Murray, Eddie Burke, Murray Laird, Harold Lyons, Albert Hudson, the Rev'd Mr. Dunlop and the Rev'd J. Maxwell.

In charge of the various groups were Aubrey Hudson, as Scouter, Doreen Jolley as Girl Guide Captain, Doreen Hazel as Brown Owl, and M. Coupland Akela of the Wolf Cubs. Later assistants with the Cubs were Agnes van Vliet, Maureen Needham and Mollie Pomeroy.

The Cubs were a total delight. We had great kids in the Pack and had so many good times, hikes, scavenger hunts, picnics, and Fairs where their badge work was on display. The picture on page 160 at the beginning of this chapter shows most of the Pack after a combined scavenger hunt and picnic. Those bags they are carrying are not sandwiches and cookies; they contain fishworms, assorted bugs, leaves, feathers, horse hair, coloured stones, barks and mosses. For dinner that day, every Cub brought one raw egg and we fried the eggs and made our own sandwiches, with ketchup on the bread as well as a handful of fresh watercress from the creek behind the rock. Homemade cookies topped it off. Mrs. Elsie Collis, a Brampton Cub leader, was a tremendous help in getting the 1ST Norval Pack off to a good start.

In the picture on page 160 are: (top row on the rock, left to right) Laurie Reed, Gordon Brain, Howard Chester, Peter van Vliet, Ken Richardson, Guy Wellington, Ron Scondo, Charlie Carney and Barry Cleave. Bottom row — Ross Cunningham, Tommy Hunter, Ronnie McLean, Bill Richardson, Peter Pomeroy, Bob Bidwell, Dave Fendley, Carl Sedore, Bill Donaldson, Sandy Barnes and Alan Fendley.

Upper Canada College and Others Camping out in Norval

For the past seventy years Norval has been given a unique opportunity to introduce itself to thousands of young people from all over the country, and also from abroad. The west end Y.M.C.A. from Toronto established a campground adjoining the village on land purchased for them by Mr. Morden Neilson in 1928. Their outdoor swimming pool was state of the art for the times, the very best.

As a sad footnote to the above, just this year (1997) a real estate developer has been given permission to go ahead with some very ambitious plans for that beautiful property.

Around 1912 Upper Canada College of Toronto purchased

525 acres from the Robert Noble estate, just north of the village, with the intention of relocating the College from its site on Avenue Road. The playing fields were to be the flat ten acres beside the river and the school was marked out on the hills on the crest of the Credit Valley. "Old Boys" of the College were invited to a picnic on the proposed site, and on arrival at the Grand Trunk Station at Norval were met with carriages and transported all around the impressive piece of property the College had bought.

However, when war broke out in 1914, everything was put on hold. The aftermath of the war in the 1920s, followed by the stock market crash in 1929 and the ten years of Depression in the 1930s seemed to signal the end of College plans at Norval. During the 1930s a Chicago business man offered $75,000 for the entire acreage, but decided it was too far into the backwoods and lost interest. Thank Heaven for that!

In 1938, Alan Stephen, Headmaster of the Prep School at Upper Canada, and his second in command, Alan Harris, felt that the property was a golden opportunity to create an outdoor addition to city classes. To that end a bungalow, already established on the property, was converted into a small lodge with bunk beds for students. This served them well until Stephen House was built. "Stephen House" was so named in honour of Alan Stephen, Headmaster from 1934 to 1966.

In 1938 Dad was approached by the Board of the College

Alan Stephen, Headmaster of Upper Canada College and my Dad at a reforestation programme on the shool's Norval property.

about the carpentry involved in converting the bungalow, and in the following May, 1939, the first "Norval Picnic and Tree Planting Day" was celebrated on the grounds. From then on Charlie was consulted on all matters concerning the Norval property, from building a foot-bridge over the river to preparing the various fields for reforestation. The picnics are still a popular event for students, parents, and neighbours of the College.

One of the best things about the College's renewed interest in their property was a reforestation project. It started in 1939 when 12,000 trees were planted, many of them by the students, and the practice continued for years. Over a million forest trees now cover the hills and parts of the valley. The orchard was replaced by an arboretum, and named in honour of Alan Harris, a loved and respected Master in the Prep.

Camp Robogi (Rotary boys and girls) half a mile below the village was not a long term camp, but an enjoyable one.

The Neighbourhood Workers Association of Toronto, who looked after underprivileged children, camped on the Pinecrest hill above the village for brief periods.

The Girl Guides camped on the Credit flats at different periods over the years and in the late 1920s held a Camporee there for several hundred Guides.

In the 1920s Colonel Noble offered the use of his large home to the United Church, which operated a hostel for boys from the British Isles who wanted to come to Canada. The boys were given a break on their passage if they were willing to work on a farm for a year or so. Mr. Alex McLaren of Georgetown was in charge of the arrangements and Miss Farmer of Georgetown was the Matron.

The Nobles had wanted to live in Toronto while their daughters were in University, and when the girls were through their courses, the Colonel and his wife came back home. Their generosity in sharing the use of their home was much appreciated by those immigrant boys.

The Lacrosse pad on the school grounds in Norval was erected in 1946 and was well used for several years. Lacrosse was a new game to most of the Norval youngsters although it was very popular in Brampton where their Excelsiors were the Canadian champions.

THE NORVAL WOMEN'S INSTITUTE

The Women's Institute has been a part of the fabric of the Norval community for almost one hundred years. By following the principles laid down by Mrs. Adelaide Hoodless to improve the quality of life for rural women, whole communities have benefited. The motto of the Women's Institute has always been "For Home and Country." They have sponsored Junior Institutes, have been quick to help fire victims or anyone in need, have made donations to charities, provided assistance and scholarships for students, and held home workshops for cooking, sewing etc. One of their interests has been in restoring neglected pioneer cemeteries.

In 1935 when Lord and Lady Tweedsmuir arrived at Government House in Ottawa, he as Governer-General, Lady Tweedsmuir suggested a project that the Women's Institutes were quick to adopt; that of recording the pioneer families of the area for future historians. The project also involved keeping abreast of special community events as they happened, and recording them as well. There are now literally hundreds of volumes of community histories all across the country, of which most are now on microfilm in libraries. A mother-lode of information for people wanting to trace their roots has been created. It is a genealogist's treasure chest! The local custodians of the Tweedsmuir histories have been Marion (Noble) Reed, Gwen May, Dorothy (Watson) McLean, and Norma Thompson; every one of them are of local pioneer stock themselves.

Lady Tweedsmuir was an author in her own right. She wrote under the pen-name of "O. Douglas." *Penny Plain* was one of her books. Lord Tweedsmuir was a noted author too, writing as "John Buchan." His books were mysteries like, *The Thirty-nine Steps*.

The first President of the Norval Institute was Mrs. Alex Noble. During the first World War the members knitted socks, mitts and scarves for the Canadians overseas. The socks had to be knitted with a "Kitchener Toe" and special knitting instructions were sent to the Institute branches. There is no seam over the toe in a "Kitchener" sock, named for Lord Kitchener who perhaps had delicate feet. We had one of those instruction pamphlets around the house for years.

> *1997 is the 100TH Anniversary of the Women's Institute. Our Hearty Congratulations on their many achievements.*

Spencer Wilson

Spencer Wilson, resident on the Ninth Line and a descendant of the pioneer Wilson Family of 1840, has a unique hobby that has benefited many families, not only around Norval but for miles in every direction. Spencer can witch for water. He is a water diviner, or a dowser. His grandfather had the same ability;

Spencer considers his craft is a gift and he has been using it for about 50 years.

His tools are very simple, a sturdy forked twig from a willow or an apple tree, or even a v-shaped wire. His record for finding a good spring for a new well is 100%.

Dowsing has been practiced for centuries and is still used as a serious method of finding water, minerals, pipes, cables, etc. When camping one summer at Bon Echo Park on Mazinaw Lake, the caretaker of the park told us he used willow to find water and maple to find mineral. Dowsing has been credited with filling the gap when modern technology has failed and has proved to to be more accurate than some of the modern so-called treasure trackers. Call it witching, divining or dowsing, it does work, but how it works is a question as yet unanswered.

Many theories have been put forward, the strongest of which is the theory of the "earth force," which is an abstract name for the earth's magnetic field.

The earth force theory might also have a bearing on how birds migrate and return to the home area. Their homing instincts defy most explanations but come home they do.

The Short Course

In January 1933, Peel County Agricultural Representatives sponsored a four-week Short Course in St. Paul's Parish Hall. Speakers were brought in and topics of farm and home interest were discussed, as well as livestock and veterinary problems. The girls enjoyed workshops on sewing, cooking, nutrition and fashions.

After a lecture on "Money and Management," Joe Tisdale said "Pardon me, Sir, you omitted one thing. How and where do we get the money to manage?" Good question. The Depression already had a stranglehold on the country.

At least twice a week the boys' class would be taken to various farms to judge all kinds of dairy and beef herds, pigs, horses, sheep and chickens. After one such tour the class was asked "What is the best way to keep milk?" Said Jimmie Eccles, "In the cow."

Every Friday afternoon was a social and fun time with entertainment and Spelling and Geography matches. Exams were written at the end of the course, and on the final evening a banquet was held, certificates were handed out and howlers from the exam papers were read, to the great amusement of all.

The Short Courses held all cross the Province gave farm families a chance to share in a general knowledge of agriculture as it was taught in an Agricultural College. The leaders for the course in Norval were Jim Shearer, Ag. Rep. for Peel County, Ed Binkley, Horticulturist, and several members of the Women's Institute. There was even a little orchestra that everyone enjoyed: Donald Bull on violin, Mac Watson, guitar, George (Sparky) Bignell on the mouthorgan and Dorothy Watson chording on the piano.

January 1933 was a happy month for all who attended the course, and for the farm kids it broke the back of a long winter.

CHAPTER NINE

The Pioneers Live On

The influence of the whole community that we know as Norval has extended into every area of public life in this country: the medical field, the arts and letters fraternity, the teaching and nursing professions, the diplomatic and political arenas, the geological and theological world and in music, agriculture, military service, and every conceivable trade.

The Robert Noble connection alone produced seven doctors, several nurses, teachers, lawyers, accountants, a geologist and a Federal M.P.

Robert's son, Dr. R.T. Noble, was head of the Academy of Medicine for years, and his son, Dr. Clark Noble, worked with Doctors Frederick Banting and Charlie Best in the discovery of insulin. Dr. Clark Noble is buried in Norval.

Dr. Robert Noble's third son, Dr. R.L. Noble, spent his life in cancer research and developed the only known help for childhood leukemia at that time, Vincristine and Vinblastine, extracts from a *Madagascar vinca* (periwinkle). He died of cancer himself, aged 82, and is buried in Norval.

Local farmers are well known for the excellence of their herds, and their cattle have been shipped around the world to reinforce agricultural practices, especially in the Third World.

Strangely, the pioneering spirit is still very much alive in the Norval area. The early settlers would be happy to know that so many of their grandchildren and great-grandchildren still live on their home acres, but have turned their talents and the land in new directions. A partial list of pioneers who are "still here" includes the Clarks (1818), the Whaleys (1819), the Dolsons (1817), the McNabs (1820), the Leslies (1823), the Lairds (early 1833), the McClures (1831), the Wilsons (1840), the Eccles (1842), the Lyons (1835), the Laidlaws (1840), the Glendinnings

(1860s), the Birds (1860s), the Nobles (1860s), the Watsons (1840s), the Mays (1834), the Earlys (1820), the Fiddlers (1869), the Hustlers (1822) and the Hyatts (1812). Jim Clark is still living in the "new home" of 1888, built by the Laird brothers. Gordon Sharpe is still living on the edge of the old home place, which sat next to ours.

The Apple Factory, on the corner of the fourth line, Chinguacousy (now Mississauga Road) and #7 highway, was just an empty corner until Roy Laidlaw put up a small building where he could sell apples from their farm. It all started when Cliff Laidlaw, Roy's eldest son, developed allergies to hay and straw, so for him there could be no future with the Holstein herd. As Cliff said, "When a cow kicks you, you're out of there!" Cliff's farm interest was in the orchard, so his dad decided that a small market for their produce was the answer. In 1979 that little apple market was opened, and has grown incredibly. It is truly a Laidlaw family business with all hands on deck.

Crawford's Bakery and Food Shop began when Murry Laird gave his daughter, Elaine, and her husband Bob Crawford, acreage off the original Laird Homestead. In 1967 they started selling produce out of a farm wagon parked near the highway, and also that year Bob put up one-third of the eventual market building. Bob also grew roses in greenhouses he had built, but found rose culture was too time consuming. Now, fresh bread and chocolate truffles have been added to Elaine's delicious pies. Many specialty foods are on the shelves and great lunches are served in the Atrium Café on week-ends.

Carl Laidlaw and Sons, on the fifth line Chinguacousy, changed their farm and stable from cattle to a farm market and grew the produce they wanted to sell. This too has been a very successful venture. As a sideline they have an herb garden with accommodations for drying and preserving the herbs and making herb vinegars and herb jellies. A delightful spot to visit.

And a little further south on the fifth line are the four Ferri brothers: Mac, Al, Nick and Quint. They came about 1933 with their four sisters and have contributed so much to the good of the community. They were the first growers to plant large acreages of strawberries as pick-your-own patches, and apples too.

Maple Lodge, on the old town line (now Winston Churchill Boulevard) at Whaley's Corners, is without a doubt the biggest player in the local economy. It got started in 1950, with farmers Jack and Bob May gathering up local eggs in an old truck and selling them on the streets of Toronto. Very shortly their customers were asking for fresh chicken, and the business was born. The first egg-grading station was in Jack and Jean May's living-room. By 1955, the egg and chicken trade had expanded to the point where the cattle had to move out, and offices were set up in the barns. The rest is history. Today, the plant processes 250,000 chickens a day, enough to bogle your mind. And there is a second plant in New Brunswick, managed by one of their first employees from the 1950s, John Feenstra.

As a sideline on the home market stand, the Mays have greenhouses with fresh tomatoes and lettuce, also fresh vegetables and fruit, and an excellent choice in fresh chicken.

On the fourth line, (Mississauga Road) Jim Eccles established the Eccles Elevator Company for drying grain, and went from there to become a farmer's supply centre. Jim started the business in 1975, and one of his daughters has carried on.

The same progressive, independent pioneer spirit that brought Norval's early settling families to establish themselves in this valley on the Credit River is still alive and well in the descendants of those first few.

"Nunc Dimittis"

For the past fifty years there has been another side to my life, where the joys and the sorrows, the highs and the lows in other peoples' lives took precedence over anything that was happening in my own life. My husband, my dear friend and companion, is an Anglican priest, now retired from parish duties and administration problems, but still active in his calling. We are fortunate to have two dear daughters, Laurie and Mary Jean. The years have been good to us and we have survived, having encountered only minor aggravations inherent in any life of public service. We could never repay all of the kindness everyone has shown to us over a lifetime.

Countless times over all those years I have heard my husband repeat this most beautiful prayer from "The Book of Common Prayer," the book with four hundred years of tradition behind it — this prayer for all the people, for the end of a day, or for the end of a life:

> *"O Lord, support us all the day long in this troublous life, until the shadows lengthen and the evening comes, the busy world is hushed, and the fever of life is over and our work is done. Then, Lord, in Thy mercy, grant us safe lodging, a holy rest, and peace at the last, through Jesus Christ our Lord. Amen."*